A Mandate for Playful Learning in Preschool

A Mandate for Playful Learning in Preschool

PRESENTING THE EVIDENCE

Kathy Hirsh-Pasek, Roberta Michnick Golinkoff,
Laura E. Berk, and Dorothy G. Singer

UNIVERSITY PRESS

2009

OXFORD
UNIVERSITY PRESS

Oxford University Press, Inc., publishes works that further
Oxford University's objective of excellence
in research, scholarship, and education.

Oxford New York

Auckland   Cape Town   Dar es Salaam   Hong Kong   Karachi
Kuala Lumpur   Madrid   Melbourne   Mexico City   Nairobi
New Delhi   Shanghai   Taipei   Toronto

With offices in
Argentina   Austria   Brazil   Chile   Czech Republic   France   Greece
Guatemala   Hungary   Italy   Japan   Poland   Portugal   Singapore
South Korea   Switzerland   Thailand   Turkey   Ukraine   Vietnam

Published by Oxford University Press, Inc.
198 Madison Avenue, New York, New York 10016

www.oup.com

Oxford is a registered trademark of Oxford University Press

Library of Congress Cataloging-in-Publication Data

A mandate for playful learning in preschool : presenting
the evidence / Kathy Hirsh-Pasek . . . [et al.].
p. cm.
Includes bibliographical references and index.
ISBN 978-0-19-538271-6   1. Play.   2. Learning.   3. Early childhood
education.   I. Hirsh-Pasek, Kathy.
LB1137.M23 2009
372.21—dc22

                                                        2008032420

9 8 7 6 5 4 3 2

Printed in the United States of America
on acid-free paper

We dedicate this book to all the preschool educators, Head Start teachers, principals, policy makers, children's museum staff, librarians, pediatricians, and parents who have shared their concerns with us about the present educational regime as we have traveled around the country. In particular, it is for the 500-plus educators who wanted to attend our conference called PLAY = LEARNING at Yale University in 2005. We hope this piece is helpful to teachers of young children who have told us repeatedly that they needed a statement like this to affirm what they know is best for young children . . .

We also dedicate this book to Professor Edward Zigler of Yale University who has spent his career championing children's right to learn through play . . .

Finally, we dedicate this book to Laura's son, David Berk, who served as our participant observer, sharing his concerns from the trenches.

Acknowledgments

This paper was conceived at the PLAY = LEARNING Conference held at Yale University in June of 2005. We are grateful to Stanley and Debra Lefkowitz for their support of Hirsh-Pasek's research and to the late Maryanne Bowers of the University of Delaware for her tireless work on bibliographic sources. We also express our appreciation to Catharine Carlin and Mallory Jensen of Oxford University Press for their unstinting support, and to Catherine Tamis-LeMonda and Carol Vukelich who were kind enough to give us feedback on our policy recommendations. Grants from the National Science Foundation (BCS-0642529) and the National Institutes of Health (5R01HD050199) were instrumental in supporting the first two authors.

Hirsh-Pasek: khirshpa@temple.edu; fax: 610–642–5275
Golinkoff: Roberta@udel.edu; fax: 302–831–4110
Berk: leberk@ilstu.edu
Singer: dorothy.singer@yale.edu

Foreword

This small monograph is a much needed antidote to to-day's common approach to child development—an approach that is antithetical to the knowledge bases of both the fields of human development and early childhood education. In homes and schools across America, parents and teachers are concentrating on cognitive development, which is being treated as much more important than other human subsystems such as the social and emotional domains and even physical and mental health. The whole-child approach, which focuses on nurturing growth in these subsystems in addition to the intellectual sphere, has been replaced by the cognitive child. The result is that in many schools, kindergarten no longer contains blocks or dress-up corners but instead has flash cards and workbooks. Elementary schools are abandoning recess and gym because administrators think they take time from productive learning activities. Even at home, parents are loading up on toys, DVDs, and electronics that have the magic word "educational" in their names. Yet children are regularly abandoning "toys that teach" when they discover that it is much more entertaining and informative to play with the boxes the toys came in.

As such behavior illustrates, a false dichotomy has been constructed between play and learning. To the child, the two activities are one and the same. This realization had its genesis in Robert White's seminal article on social competence. In his paradigm-shifting paper, White deflated the notion that external reinforcement is the main driver for learning, like doling out a treat when a child learns to count to 10 or a dollar for an "A" on a report card. White instead saw learning as motivated by the drive that all humans have from birth forward to deal with the world in a competent, effective manner (now commonly called the efficacy or mastery drive). In this view, the motivating reinforcement for learning is internal, consisting of satisfaction or sheer pleasure in being effective; this in turn results in a sense of self-worth and a desire to master yet more difficult tasks. Experts now know that as children age, reliance on external reinforcement diminishes as the mastery drive strengthens. The vehicle through which this all takes place is children's play, both spontaneous and assisted. Thus play activities are produced naturally by the mastery drive—the need to explore and "figure things out" and the good feeling from doing so.

As Vygotsky taught, social collaborators are central to the child's developmental progression. First and most important are parents whose daily interactions with the child beyond physical care are thousands of playful and emotionally appealing gestures—a game of peek-a-boo, a rough-housing, or even making silly noises or faces. Reading a book and explaining the pictures while the child is happily sitting in the parent's lap is really a form of play to the child. Later, other children and adults will be partners in play, and the play itself will move to higher levels of learning, as when children progress from rolling a ball across the floor to organized sports, or from simple four-piece drop-in puzzles to 1,000-piece interlocking murals.

The centrality of play to human development can be seen in its universality. Children play even in the most onerous situations, such as in hospitals or war zones. Young animals play. And play is important in every single developmental domain. Physical play is healthy and remains one of society's best tools in the battle against the childhood obesity epidemic of recent years. Health benefits are often noted by those who advocate for the return of both recess and physical education classes in our schools. Play also encourages fine and gross motor development. Social skills are a natural outgrowth of group play. Play is also central in emotional development. It can provide catharsis for negative experiences and help the child in emotional self-regulation. Indeed, therapeutic nursery schools for preschoolers with emotional and behavioral problems invariably are based on play practices.

In the controversy over the cognitive child versus the whole child approaches, the status of play is weighted differently. When the whole child view is in ascendancy, play activities are valued. When the emphasis is on the cognitive child, play is denigrated. In my 50 years in the field, I have witnessed this pendulum swing back and forth from one extreme to another. (See Zigler and Bishop-Josef's chapter in *Children's play: The roots of reading.*) A half century ago, when the Soviet Union beat the United States into space with the launching of the satellite Sputnik, Americans panicked. One highly visible commentator, Admiral Hiram Rickover, attributed this amazing feat to the Soviet Union's superior education system. Admiral Rickover drew a stark contrast between young children in that country "who were learning math at an early age while our children were finger painting." The response in the United States was to reemphasize the basics of reading, writing, and arithmetic. Play was out.

In the ensuing decades, the focus on the basics gradually gave way to an emphasis on self-esteem. If educators could make children feel good about themselves, their academic learning would soar. The pendulum was given a sharp whack in the other direction during the years of the George W. Bush administration. Society received a clear signal of President Bush's preference at a White House conference on children held shortly after he took office. Chaired by Mrs. Bush, the event was titled a conference on cognitive development. However, it turned out to be much more narrow than that, targeting only a small slice of cognitive phenomena. The conference was managed by an expert on children's literacy and focused on improving reading skills through the use of phonemic and other didactic teaching.

As time went on, the Bush administration promulgated a plethora of policies that treated the developing child as essentially a cognitive system; like a computer, he or she is carefully programmed with skill-producing activities leading to literacy, numeracy, and other knowledge content areas. This orientation may be seen in President's Bush's Reading First program and in his Good Start, Grow Smart initiative. The centerpiece of his efforts was the No Child Left Behind Act with its emphasis on academic testing. Education in many schools has become little more than coaching for tests, taking tests, and reviewing test results. The Bush administration also made an orchestrated effort to abandon Head Start's whole child, comprehensive service approach and turn the 40-year-old institution into primarily a literacy program. When this failed, he imposed the National Reporting System, which required standardized testing of Head Start preschoolers. It is no wonder, then, that play has come under attack in our preschools, elementary schools, and even children's homes.

It is time for a reconciliation between the two conceptualizations of the child. Respected thinkers are now speaking of combining the intentional learning of the child by embedding academic activities into play activities. See, for example, the play-based curriculum of Bodrova and Leong as well as the recent statements by Deborah Stipek, the Dean of Stanford University's School of Education and a noted expert on preschool education. The excellent contribution to understanding the significance of children's play you are about to read should help move the conceptual pendulum away from the restrictive view of child development as cognitive development toward one embracing whole-child development, and with it, the encouragement of children's play.

Edward Zigler, PhD
Sterling Professor of Psychology, Emeritus
Director Emeritus, Edward Zigler Center in
Child Development and Social Policy
Yale University

Contents

A Mandate for Playful Learning
in Preschool

Executive Summary

Play has become a four-letter word. In an effort to give children a head start on academic skills such as reading and mathematics, play is discouraged and didactic learning is stressed. This book presents the scientific evidence in support of three points: (1) children need both unstructured free play and playful learning under the gentle guidance of adults to best prepare them for entrance into formal school, (2) academic and social development are so inextricably intertwined that the former must not trump attention the latter, and (3) learning and play are not incompatible—learning takes place best when children are engaged and enjoying themselves.

The book is organized into three chapters. The first describes the current crisis in preschool education and suggests that the lack of attention to play and playful learning lies at its core. We propose that there exists a false and counterproductive dichotomy between play on the one hand and learning on the other. This dichotomy is echoed in society at large as parents are influenced by the media and the marketplace to buy "educational" toys and restrict free play. Although we agree that account-ability and assessment are essential, we suggest that the current emphasis on assessment in higher grades has led to narrowly defined curricula objectives in the preschool. Curriculum development has been more responsive to the practical constraints of assessment than to the find-ings of evidence-based pedagogy.

The second chapter presents the evidence that play and playful learning enhance academic, social, and emotional outcomes in preschool. Playful learning, and not drill-and-practice, engages and motivates children in ways that enhance developmental outcomes and lifelong learn-ing. After defining play and playful learning, we examine assumptions about how children learn and suggest that preschools are no longer teaching the "whole" child. The weight of the evidence, from random assignment to corre-lational to interventional studies, suggests that both free play and playful learning create optimal environments for achievement. In addition, children in developmentally ap-propriate classrooms often show less anxiety and stronger social skills.

The epilogue moves from data to application, present-ing seven principles that are derived from the science that informs preschool pedagogy. These principles reflect consensus across the learning sciences for how children learn best. If followed, these principles can contribute to the creation of preschools that are equipped to educate the work force and citizenry of the 21st century.

Finally, the book ends with a set of recommendations for policy makers. These recommendations are designed to translate the findings from the research into building excellent preschool programs that encourage family and community participation.

If we hope to prepare intelligent, socially skilled, cre-ative thinkers for the global workplace of tomorrow, we must return play and playful learning to their rightful position in children's lives.

ONE

What Happened to Playful Learning in Preschool?

Imagine a school for 3-year-olds in which there are no pictures on the walls, no toys on the floor, and no children making noise. Is this a school in a third world country with severely limited resources? Or, perhaps a school for children with some rare medical syndrome who cannot tolerate the stimulation appropriate for typical 3-year-olds? It is neither of these. It is instead a preschool in Florida where parents pay for their children to be taught five different languages.

This inappropriately intensive preschool, and others like it, demonstrates how far society has gone astray in early childhood education and how badly misled many parents are. At a time when children should be experimenting with making shapes in clay and building towers only to crash them, we have created an environment in which children are drilled and practiced like parrots in a circus act. Learning another language is a wonderful gift. But this is not how second languages are learned; they are learned in the nexus of social interaction, during everyday activities and in the context of meaningful relationships.[1]

The example above may not be one that occurs in profusion, but early childhood programs today have many more didactic components than they did 20 years ago.[2] Didactic teaching of the body of academic facts deemed essential for "success" in today's schools is squeezing out developmentally appropriate education in the early years, the cornerstone of which is rich, playful experiences aimed at developing the whole child. As forewarned by Sigel, the use of "hot-housing" techniques to foster early childhood learning has led to a societal focus on structured activities designed to promote academic results rather than the playful learning that engenders the same outcomes but with the added value of thinking and creativity.[3]

HOW DID WE GET HERE?

The didactic focus in preschools comes from two main sources. The first is a societal misconception—fueled by overstated claims about brain growth and rooted perhaps in economic uncertainty—about what it takes for children to succeed in school. Parents feel pressure as never before to accelerate and augment their children's learning.[4] They have been bombarded with exaggerated and scientifically suspect information about how the majority of brain development is more or less over by 5 years of age.[5] The marketplace has been happy to follow along, providing parents with the opportunity to purchase any number of questionable "brain growth" electronic toys whose efficacy is far from established.[6] The onus is on middle-class parents to do everything they can to nurture their children's intelligence as early as possible. Preschool directors who know better often feel the pressure to succumb to requests for worksheets and less unstructured, "time-wasting" play.

A second reason for didactic preschools is in response to the fact that children from underprivileged environments are less ready for the transition to school than are their middle-class peers. This long-established fact was brought to the attention of the American people in a genuine, bipartisan attempt to close the persistent "achievement gap" in our country. Based on strong scientific evidence, it was known that intervening during the preschool years could reduce the gap and help poor children reach their potential.[7] These goals were laudable. They gave birth to the No Child Left Behind Act of 2001 (Public Law 107–110; hereafter NCLB; http://www.ed.gov/nclb/landing.jhtml) and its counterpart Good Start, Grow Smart—its companion Early Childhood Initiative (http://www.whitehouse.gov/infocus/earlychildhood/toc.html). Yet many less advantaged 3- to 5-year-old children had no preschool experience. Furthermore, when they did, there was huge variability in the quality of these experiences.[8] Therefore, the calls to teach more content in the early years and to educate teachers to meet learning standards were sounded widely.

There is virtual consensus that preschool children benefit from learning *content.* This is especially true for underprivileged children who do not obtain "school-ready" information in everyday activities such as daily reading or playing board games. These children need curricula that provide them with learning opportunities that build reading, mathematics, and social skills. Importantly, the field of early childhood education also knows something about how to create these outstanding preschool environments and what skills children need to succeed.[9] For example, early literacy rests on the ability to recognize and distinguish between letters and their sounds, to know that books convey useful information, and to understand that the pages should be turned from right to left but the letters interpreted from left to right.[10]

The same is true in the area of mathematics. Many studies have probed the kinds of knowledge that middle-class children bring to school with them, as if for free, because their parents and caregivers talk to them about numbers and provide them with numerical experiences.[11] Children who engage in numerical games that challenge them to add and subtract and to think beyond what they know are better prepared for school.[12] Even games such as "Chutes and Ladders" have been shown to provide children with the kinds of informal learning opportunities they need to build on for success in school mathematics.[13]

In addition, abundant research exists on the importance of *social skills* for success in school. "Whole" children attend school; they don't just send their brains along. Nurturing children's social and emotional skills in preschool enables them to profit from school instruction. Children who thrive in preschool are prepared to become members of a classroom community where the individual's needs come after the needs of the group—a tough lesson for young children. Children who do well in preschool listen to directions, pay attention, solve disputes with words, and focus on tasks without constant supervision. Recent research suggests that they learn these skills through playful activities.[14]

Educators know how to create high-quality preschool classrooms that contribute to narrowing the achievement gap. Burgeoning research is even addressing the best ways to assess what young children learn. Good assessments focus on integrative and dynamic techniques that comprehensively capture the nature of children's learning, minimize validity concerns related to context and culture, and evaluate how competencies in different developmental domains interact for optimal learning.[15] *Accountability and assessment are crucial components of any educational enterprise.* When done well, and according to scientific principles, assessments inform us about how individual children are doing. They also provide sensitive teachers with much useful information about where children need help.

There is, then, wide agreement that accountability is necessary and that school readiness—especially for low-income children—requires exposure to a rich preschool curriculum. Where there is contention, however, is in how to best deliver that curriculum. Here we review the scientific evidence suggesting that *how you learn is as important as what you learn* and that successful programs are those that encourage playful learning where children are actively engaged in meaningful discovery. In the wake of NCLB and its downward extension, we are spending so much time focused narrowly on the content that we are losing our perspective on how to best educate the next generation.

SACRIFICING GOOD PEDAGOGY FOR CURRICULAR GOALS: THE FALSE DICHOTOMY BETWEEN PLAY AND LEARNING

As NCLB took hold in the primary grades, preschool classrooms replaced playful learning with practice and drill. Blocks were replaced with worksheets. Both free play and playful learning declined precipitously in U.S. preschools, where they were sidelined as an expendable diversion in favor of early preparation for school test-taking. According to a recent statement in the *Wall Street Journal,* "President Bush's No Child Left Behind program pushed districts to require more from younger pupils. As a result, in many districts, skills once deemed appropriate for first or second graders are being taught in kindergarten, while kindergarten skills have been bumped down to preschool."[16] In response, increasing numbers of preschools and kindergartens reduced their play periods or eliminated them entirely.[17] As one teacher wrote, "I am an ex–Bronx New York City third grade teacher who is so sad about the lack of thinking and learning . . . in many schools. One of my most crushing memories was just a year ago, when I saw and heard bags of large wooden blocks being tossed in the garbage. I tried very hard to make a difference in the thoughtfulness of the teachers and administration. But I was a very solo voice."

This demise of play in early childhood programs has been virtually formalized in the largest U.S. early-intervention program serving low-income children. The 2003 congressional reauthorization of Head Start brought an end to program evaluations that included assessments of children's social and emotional functioning and, instead, accentuated attention to preliteracy and premath skills. This shift took place in the face of virulent criticisms from early-childhood experts about the risks of narrowing Head Start's focus to academic training—an emphasis unsupported by research findings on how young children actually learn.[18]

Similar moves are afoot in England. Its new early-years foundation stage framework (EYFS) would affect all nurseries and kindergartens. The system would require children to be continually assessed according to 13 different learning scales, including writing, problem solving, and numeracy.[19] As in the United States, experts are sounding research-based pleas for developmentally based curricular decisions that take into account children's psychosocial well-being.[20]

Despite an extensive research literature that clarifies the components of excellent, effective early education through playful learning,[21] U.S. preschools and kindergartens are becoming academic "boot camps." In response, increasing numbers of young children are failing to meet the inappropriate standards set for them. In Texas, since 1993, when standardized testing was instituted as a means toward improving public school performance, the number of kindergarten students who were held back has been growing steadily each year.[22] In 1994 to 1995, 1.5% of kindergartners were held back, compared with 2.5% in 1998 to 1999 and 3.7% in 2003 to 2004. Academically regimented classrooms, with their repetitive, boring tasks that exceed the attention spans and patience of 3- to 5-year-olds, frequently engender withdrawal, rebellion, and emotional "meltdowns." These behavior problems are believed to contribute to a rising tide of expulsions in U.S. preschools.[23] The Foundation for Child Development's "Prekindergartners Left Behind" revealed that preschools are expelling students for unmanageable behavior at three times the rate of public schools (6.7 versus 2.1 per thousand, respectively). About 4.5 times as many boys as girls, as well as twice as many African Americans as white or Latino children, are being made to leave.[24] The report expressed concern that preschool failure might launch these vulnerable children—who are most in need of comprehensive preschool enrichment—on a tragic path of educational failure at a very young age.

BEYOND THE CLASSROOM: PRESCHOOL PRESSURE AT HOME

At least for middle-class children, the pressures that kindergarten and preschool are engendering are also spilling over into the home. Many parents, concerned about the high-stakes tests their children must endure, seek to help their children succeed through alternative means. Preschool tutoring programs have become a multibillion dollar business as parents attempt to equip their preschoolers with basic skills in reading, writing, and mathematics.[25] The $20-billion educational toy industry has also profited from society's insatiable appetite for anything that presumably gives children an advantage.[26]

Often to children's detriment, the marketplace has had an impact on what parents consider play. As the historian Howard Chudacoff argues, play used to be spontaneous and child-driven.[27] Since the 1950s when toys were first advertised on television, "commercial toys have almost completely colonized children's free time, [while] for most of history, play primarily meant roaming around the countryside or improvising with objects found or made at home."[28] Now parents buy an inordinate number of toys,[29] with "techno" toys leading the list.[30] Yet Elkind argues[31] and our own work agrees[32] that "techno toys" may reduce the, " . . . imaginative activity [that] is the basis of creativity in the arts and sciences." Too many toys—and especially too many electronic toys—may dampen children's make-believe play as well as stifle their curiosity about how things work.

Parents' beliefs about the nature of play are both driven by and influence the marketplace. Indeed, their very definition of play differs from those of child development experts. Recent work indicates that although experts are more likely to consider *unstructured* activities to be play, parents are more likely to consider interaction with computerized, electronic toys that demand one right answer to be a kind of play.[33]

The demise of unstructured playtime is not an American phenomenon. Singer, Singer, D'Agostino, and Mallikarjum conducted a study that involved 2,400 interviews of parents with children younger than 12 years of age from Argentina, Brazil, China, France, India, Indonesia, Ireland, Morocco, Pakistan, Portugal, South Africa, Thailand, Turkey, the United Kingdom, the United States, and Vietnam.[34] Across the globe, parents report that children are growing up "too fast." Children are increasingly being denied opportunities to take part in unstructured activities as well as to learn from their own curiosity and exploration.

Parents' beliefs about preschool children's needs seem to be increasingly conflicted. Many modern parents do not seem to appreciate the value of free play and gently guided play for children's learning. Rather, parents' buying patterns are consistent with the belief that electronic toys can teach children their ABCs. Paradoxically, play with electronic toys has no proven educational value for infants, toddlers, and preschoolers, as the Kaiser Foundation report on media products for young children made patently clear.[35] Recent findings from our research bear this out.[36] Electronic console books are found in 90% of American homes and more than 100,000 classrooms. Yet when parents and their 3-year-olds read an electronic console book together, parents spend much of the time trying to control their child's manipulation of the book rather than talking about the story. With electronic books, 41% of the parent's talk is about managing the child's book behavior and only 59% is about the story itself. With traditional books, 92% of parent's talk is about the story. Not surprisingly, children understand significantly more about the story when they hear it from a traditional book than when they hear the electronic version. Years of literacy research have taught us that one of the best predictors of reading success are the conversations parents and children have about traditional storybooks, where parent and child jointly elaborate on story content and where sound effects are produced by the parent and the child.[37] Children pick up new vocabulary without even trying as parents talk about what the child's finger points out. With traditional books, children are not preoccupied with the "bells and whistles" but with following the story's narrative, a skill that is crucial for learning and loving to read.

Yet another way in which the preschool academic emphasis manifests itself in society is in the rise of specialized classes for young children and in preschools dedicated to teaching children a particular skill. Computer science is now a preschool subject, along with formal reading instruction, Chinese, music, and acrobatics. Classes with these names abound in our communities. Touted as a way for parents to "enrich" their children's learning and pave the way for their academic success, such lessons have families rushing back and forth in the car instead of communicating, interacting, and most importantly, playing.

The depletion of informal, playful learning in young children's lives is so profound that the American Academy of Pediatrics recently felt compelled to issue a "white paper" on play written by Kenneth Ginsberg and a distinguished committee.[38] It is surprising indeed when a professional society dedicated to children's well-being sees an urgent need to create guidelines to help their members encourage children's play. As Ginsberg and his committee wrote, "This report offers guidelines on how pediatricians can advocate for children by helping families, school systems, and communities consider how best to ensure play is protected. . . ."[39] It is time to restore that balance.

TURNING BACK THE TIDE

What is needed are preschools that impart necessary content through playful learning and provide time for the spontaneous free play that is so crucial to social-emotional and academic growth. As Henig wrote:

> Scientists who study play, in animals and humans alike, are developing a consensus view that play is something more than a way for restless kids to work off steam; more than a way for chubby kids to burn off calories; more than a frivolous luxury. Play . . . is a central part of neurological growth and development—one important way that children build complex, skilled, responsive, socially adept and cognitively flexible brains.[40]

Young children the world over feel compelled to play, often with a degree of absorption and level of maturity rarely seen in their everyday, nonplay activities.[41] Indeed, play is omnipresent in the lives of all young primates and most young mammals—a reality that underscores its long evolutionary history and adaptive value.[42] Perhaps this is why eminent child development theorists, including Erik Erikson, Jean Piaget, and Lev Vygotsky, attached great importance to the role of play in children's development, and hundreds of studies have established that play—both spontaneous and adult-guided—are vital catalysts for intellectual, linguistic, emotional, social, moral, motor, and creative development.

It is time to stop making the false dichotomy between "play" and "education." Education for young children should resemble play, with children delighting in acquiring knowledge and skills in ways that make them feel competent and capable. Emphasis on drilling in basic skills—to the exclusion of attending to thinking, reasoning, problem solving, and emotional and social skills—does not serve children well. Children in the 21st century need not only basic skills but the ability to go beyond the facts—to synthesize, integrate, create, and evaluate. They also need to collaborate and lead effectively to achieve significant innovation and change.

The weight of the extant, large literature is clear: Children learn best through play. In this book we review the evidence that speaks to the power of playful learning for preschool children. Children should become lifelong learners, not fact-memorizers. Here we demonstrate why children need both free play and guided, playful learning to best prepare for the entrance into formal schooling.

TWO

The Evidence for Playful Learning in Preschool

Education is not the filling of a pail,
but the lighting of a fire

—W. B. Yeats

In 1969, the poet Robert Frost wrote, "Most of the change we think we see in life is due to truths being in and out of favor."[1] Nowhere is this more evident than in discussions about the role of playful learning in preschool. In their review of the history of educational trends in America, Zigler and Bishop-Josef illustrated ebbs and flows in the philosophy of preschool education as it moved back and forth from a more narrow and less playful academic focus to a playful, whole-child social approach.[2] In caricature, the former emphasized the use of drill and practice for learning facts (such as numbers and letters) and is associated with *direct-instruction* pedagogy. The latter suggested the use of playful exchanges (such as story time and block play)—an approach associated with *developmentally appropriate* pedagogy. These dichotomous views of learning dominated the landscape of early childhood education as we moved into the era of NCLB and the resultant preschool pedagogy.

In this chapter, we first examine the philosophical view of childhood that underlies these dichotomous educational practices. The empty-vessel view is consistent with the direct-instruction approach, whereas the whole-child view is consistent with the developmentally appropriate approach. Evidence in favor of the whole-child view is followed by definitions of play and playful learning. Based on classroom research, we argue that free play and playful learning, as exemplified in developmentally appropriate pedagogy, improves children's school readiness in two broad domains: cognitive skills (literacy, math, problem solving, imagination, and creativity) and social and emotional skills. The old dichotomy between developmentally appropriate versus direct instruction is crumbling as newer experimental programs incorporate elements of both philosophies and practices.

TWO EXTREME VIEWS OF CHILDREN'S DEVELOPMENT

The **empty-vessel** caricature sees preschoolers as blank slates ready to be filled with adult-provided knowledge.[3] Teachers become environmental agents, charged with "pouring in" facts as children passively absorb information. In this view, children learn best via explicit pedagogy that is compartmentalized into reading, language, social skills, physical skills, and so on. The notion of school readiness is often limited to cognitive learning, and to only a few aspects of cognitive development at that.[4] Developmental dimensions such as physical and motor growth, social skills, or the range of skills and habits that enable children to learn in the classroom (such as the ability to sustain attention) are often not addressed.[5] In the empty-vessel view, playful learning is often relegated to the sidelines as teaching is dominated by direct-instructional practices that are characterized by teacher-directed approaches with worksheets, memorization, and drill. Sometimes the empty-vessel approach surfaces with an emphasis on brain development, although little in the burgeoning field of neuroscience supports such claims as yet.[6]

The second, opposing caricature is that of a **whole active child** who learns through discovery and exploration with the guidance and support of adults. Learning is not compartmentalized into separate domains; all learning is inextricably intertwined.[7] As Zigler wrote:

> The brain is an integrated instrument. To most people the brain means intelligence. But the brain mediates emotional and social development. Emotions and cognition are constantly interwoven in the lives of children.[8]

This view suggests that the whole child integrates both cognitive and emotional information in meaningful ways with the help of a rich environment and a supportive adult.[9] This view presupposes that children seek meaning in all they do and that through play they not only practice and hone their social skills but engage in cognitive acts that expand their repertoires. Play is a prominent and integrative experience in which young children use both social and academic skills. Thus, scientists such as Roskos and Christie,[10] Zigler and Bishop-Josef,[11] and Singer, Golinkoff, and Hirsh-Pasek[12] make compelling arguments for the central role of play as a *medium* for promoting school readiness in a whole, active child. Children co-construct knowledge with adults who support physical, social-emotional, and cognitive development.

There is no question that children can profit from both direct instruction and playful, guided learning.[13] As the National Association for the Education of Young Children statement on developmentally appropriate practices suggests:

> Both theoretical perspectives are correct in explaining aspects of cognitive development during early childhood. Strategic teaching, of course, can enhance children's learning. Yet, direct instruction may be totally ineffective; it fails when it is not attuned to the cognitive capacities and knowledge of the child at that point in development.[14]

By way of example, Senechal suggests that preschoolers do not learn literacy skills merely by being exposed to print.[15] Rather, parents must offer guided lessons in letter knowledge as they read to their children. This guided learning, however, can be delivered in an engaging, socially embedded, and meaningful way as parents and children read books together.[16] (57).

In the current preschool climate, however, play has been dramatically reduced.[17] One compelling example comes from three studies that examined the prevalence of social pretend play in low-income, community-based child-care centers from 1982 to 2002.[18] Social pretend play for 4.5-year-olds dropped from 41% to only 9% of the observed time.[19] Commenting on similar trends, Bodrova and Leong wrote that we are witnessing "the disappearance of play from early childhood classrooms."[20] Zigler, one of the founders of Head Start, has argued that "play is under siege."[21] In what follows, we present evidence from correlational, longitudinal, and experimental studies indicating that play should have a central role in early-childhood classrooms.

WHY CONSIDER A WHOLE-CHILD APPROACH WITH PLAYFUL PRESCHOOL PEDAGOGY?

The central reason for the whole-child approach is that academic learning and social development are inextricably intertwined. That is, children's academic learning cannot be separated and compartmentalized from their social and emotional state. Children who are socially competent and who can self-regulate and communicate are more ready for school and are more successful in school than are other children. In fact, a persuasive body of research supports broadening "early elementary educational mandates for school readiness to include children's emotional and behavioral adjustment as key programmatic goals."[22]

This evaluation by Raver is buttressed by a number of studies. Social development is vitally important for children's abilities to adjust to school and to learn in kindergarten.[23] Children who entered kindergarten with prosocial styles made new friends more easily, gained peer acceptance, and formed a warm bond with their teacher. These favorable relationships predicted high achievement. In contrast, children with impulsive, argumentative, aggressive styles often established conflict-ridden relationships with teachers and peers, resulting in a dislike of school, low classroom participation, and poor achievement.[24] Furthermore, poor-quality early teacher-child relationships (especially for boys) as reported by children's kindergarten teachers were associated with academic and behavior problems for those children through eighth grade.[25] This was true even when the researchers controlled for IQ and for subsequent behavior problems.

Konold and Pianta also stress the tight connection between social competence and academic achievement.[26] Examining 964 typically developing 54-month-old children from the NICHD Study of Early Child Care and Youth Development, these authors found that there are many pathways to early academic readiness. One predictable route is through strong cognitive ability (despite these children's mild tendency to engage in some externalizing behaviors). Another perhaps surprising route is through average cognitive skills and above average social skills. These children fare better than peers who are equivalent in academic ability but are less socially competent.

Characterizing content areas as cognitive or social masks the fundamental relationships between these areas that emerge in the whole-child view. Importantly, not only do cognitive and social skills reinforce one another, but social skills can actually *lead* to better cognitive skills, especially for children with average cognitive abilities. Children with advanced social skills may be better at getting additional information from teachers, understanding others' points of view, cooperating with teachers and peers, and displaying initiative in the classroom. A large body of research documenting the predictive value of preschool children's social maturity for later school success indicates that school readiness should not be assessed just in terms of cognitive attainments but also in terms of social attainments that forecast children's adjustment to formal schooling.[27]

Educational outcomes are best when the whole active child rather than just the intellectual or the social child is the focus. It is noteworthy that the three most celebrated and widely known intervention studies—the Carolina Abecedarian Project,[28] the High/Scope Perry Preschool Project,[29] and the Chicago Child-Parent Center Project[30]—all used whole-child approaches in their successful attempts to narrow learning gaps between underprivileged and middle-class students.

Galinsky found that these three studies shared three characteristics that seemed to foster their success.[31] First, each nurtured a strong relationship between teachers/caregivers and individual children, ensuring that support of social development is on a par with support of cognitive development. Second, the children were viewed as active, experiential learners. Third, the teachers adapted the curriculum to children's individual needs. These characteristics are also embedded in the Alliance for Childhood's Call to Action on the Education of Young Children released in 2006—an alliance dedicated to bringing integrated whole-child learning back into the preschool agenda. The collected scientists and practitioners who form the governing body of the Alliance recognize that one way to achieve these goals is to encourage both free play and playful learning for young children.

Researchers have long realized that even free play fosters opportunities for building critical academic and social competencies[32] and that adult support and extension facilitates this type of play.[33] The National Association for the Education of Young Children (NAEYC) makes play a central piece in their "developmentally appropriate" learning philosophy, noting that:

> Play provides a context for children to practice newly acquired skills and also to function on the edge of their developing capacities, to take on new social roles, attempt novel or challenging tasks, and solve complex problems that they would not (or could not) otherwise do.[34]

Developmentally appropriate classrooms use knowledge about how children develop and learn at different ages along with playful learning to design curricula.

A WORKING DEFINITION OF PLAY AND PLAY-BASED LEARNING

If play offers a key way to support the learning of whole children in a developmentally appropriate way, it is essential to define play. Unfortunately, however, the definition of "play" has proven somewhat elusive in the literature. As Christie and Johnsen point out, the fact that "a lengthy list of psychological constructs has been connected with play is indicative of the richness and the ambiguity of the concept itself."[35] Recently, the field of play research has gone beyond the "play ethos" identified by Smith as "an uncritical and extreme assertion of the functional importance of play."[36] Numerous studies—indeed too many to mention here—now evaluate the effects of play in both correlational (relations between play and learning), longitudinal prospective (how early play experiences affect long-term learning) and experimental research.

Researchers generally discuss three types of play, although in practice, these often merge: (1) object play, the ways in which children explore objects, learn about their properties, and morph them to new functions; (2) pretend play (either alone or with others), variously referred to as make-believe, fantasy, symbolic, sociodramatic, or dramatic play, where children experiment with different social roles; and (3) physical or rough-and-tumble play, which includes everything from a 6-month-old's game of peek-a-boo to free play during recess.[37] Importantly, objects can serve as props in both pretend and rough-and-tumble play.

Object play has been extensively studied. In one classic experiment, Belsky and Most looked at object play in 40 children from 7 to 20 months of age.[38] They found, consistent with much theorizing in the field,[39] that play follows a distinct developmental pattern from infants *reacting* to the characteristics of objects, to *exploring* objects, to *symbolically using* objects as one object begins to stand for another (e.g., a banana for a phone).

Research also demonstrates that the characteristics of objects have an impact on the type of play in which children engage. McLoyd, for example, followed 36 low-income preschoolers from ages 3.5 to 5 years as they played in groups of three with high-structured toys (e.g., a tea set) or low-structured toys (e.g., blocks).[40] The 3-year-olds demonstrated more noninteractive pretend play with the high-structured toys than with the low-structured toys. The five-year-olds showed no differences. Dependence on objects in pretend play declined; fully 50% of the 4-year-olds pretend initiations occurred without the presence of a physical object but merely on the plane of ideas.[41]

Pretend play itself has various definitions, but Fein's review of pretend play[42] referred to it as a "theoretical construct" that describes behavior "in a simulative, non-literal, or 'as if' mode."[43] Thus, for example, pretend play occurs when familiar activities are performed with non-customary objects or in noncustomary contexts. When pretend play is social, "role enactment" occurs, as Fein points out. This is behavior in which children simulate the characteristics or behaviors of another person, inter-acting with other children through playing a role, such as a doctor or an astronaut. Because this kind of pre-tend play is a fluidly organized situation without codi-fied rules, children engage in much metacommunication about, for example, who will play what role (as in, "Will you be the teacher?") and what they will do next.[44] These metacommunications occur outside the frame of the pre-tend play scenario itself and nonetheless serve important purposes.[45] As children negotiate roles and plans, they are using their language and reasoning skills and imagi-nations, and, in creating a joint fantasy scenario, they are learning to cooperate.

For a long time, researchers believed that make-believe was simply an emergent property of increasing represen-tational capacity in the second year. That is, children would just start to engage in pretend play when they de-veloped the capacity to imagine "what if" and not take the world as it appeared. Once researchers moved from laboratory-based to more naturalistic studies, they found that make-believe is initially guided and scaffolded by parents, usually mothers. In Haight and Miller's study, for example, toddlers from middle income families were observed in their homes and followed longitudinally from 1 to 4 years of age.[46] At 12 months, make-believe play was one-sided, with almost all play episodes initiated by moth-ers. By the end of the second year, mothers and children displayed equal interest in starting make-believe, each initiating half of the pretend episodes. At 3 to 4 years, mother-toddler play preceded and prepared children for later peer play. In cultures in which adults do not play with toddlers, older siblings often assume the role of guiding and scaffolding toddlers' play.[47] That is, more expert partners (parents, caregivers, older siblings) teach children to play.[48] However, there is a fine line between expanding on pretend play and directing it. Shmuckler,[49] Fiese,[50] and Stilson and Harding[51] reported that if adults interfered too much, children's play reverted to simple, immature manipulation of toys, or stopped entirely.

Whether play centers on objects, fantasy and make-believe, or physical activity, researchers generally agree that eight features characterize ordinary play. Play (1) is pleasurable and enjoyable, (2) has no extrinsic goals, (3) is spontaneous, (4) involves active engagement, (5) is generally all-engrossing, (6) often has a private reality, (7) is nonliteral, and (8) can contain a certain element of make-believe.[52] Even these criteria for judging play have some fuzzy boundaries. For example, a mother who engages in a game of arranging letters on the refrigerator might have the extrinsic goal of "teaching her child the alphabet" even though her child is just having fun. Furthermore, when children pretend to be carpenters with oversized plastic hammers and pegs, they are still playing despite the imitation of real-world activities. Indeed, even playful curricula such as the Tools of the Mind program combine goal-oriented activities and dramatic play to modify children's executive functions and resultant social and academic skills.[53] Thus, although these characteristics of play have been mentioned widely in the literature, when play is used in instructional settings, the features of extrinsic goals, spontaneity, and private reality can be relaxed.

One study of play attempted to diagnose the necessary and sufficient features of play by determining which criteria lay people (who are not trained in child development) use to recognize play.[54] Five groups of 10 adults watched a videotape of 30 minutes of children's behavior in a preschool. They coded each shift in a focal child's activity according to one of five commonly quoted characteristics: (1) positive affect, (2) pretending or nonliterality, (3) intrinsic motivation (undertaken for its own sake), (4) flexibility, and (5) process orientation (emphasizing means over ends). Two additional groups of 10—one consisting of lay adults and the other of psychologists familiar with children's play—merely rated each videotaped behavior episode according to whether or not they thought it was play. Experienced and inexperienced raters agreed strongly on the presence or absence of play. Relationships between child activity and play ratings indicated that the strongest play indicator was *pretending (nonliterality)*; positive affect, flexibility, and process orientation also showed appreciable associations. Intrinsic motivation (activity engaged in for its own sake, not brought about by external rules or social demands) was not significantly related to play ratings. Moreover, the presence of multiple criteria strengthened the prediction of play judgments, with the combination of three criteria—nonliterality, positive affect, and flexibility—discriminating perfectly between play and nonplay episodes. Thus, free play contains a set of diverse characteristics, some of which are considered to be more central than others. In this context, it is particularly interesting that pretend play is absent in nonhumans but appears to be present in all human societies.[55] It is also interesting that these defining characteristics are evident in playful learning or guided play that is both playful and goal oriented.

WHAT IS "PLAYFUL LEARNING" OR "GUIDED PLAY"?

Playful learning or guided play actively engages children in pleasurable and seemingly spontaneous activities that encourage academic exploration and learning. Here, teachers using guided play have a set of learning goals in mind. They are subtly directive, embedding new learning into meaningful contexts that correspond with children's prior knowledge and experiences. A number of preschool models adopt this approach.

Tobin, Karasaw, and Hsueh,[56] for example, report that a form of play-based learning is characteristic in Japanese preschools, where teachers serve as astute observers of culturally adaptive social play, intervening only when necessary so that children learn social responsibility to one another. Montessori schools, too, are known for creating classrooms in which children choose from a number of playful, hands-on activities that have been prearranged by adults who serve as guides rather than directors of education. Importantly, the children might not even know that there was a learning goal in mind. Lillard and Else-Quest noted that 5-year-old, low-income, urban minority children who had attended Milwaukee Montessori schools for 2 years scored significantly higher in reading and math achievement than did children who did not win admission to the Montessori program by lottery.[57] Montessori children also outscored their non-Montessori peers on a measure of executive function assessing cognitive flexibility. The gains that children achieved in social and academic learning lasted until at least 12 years of age.

In further support of the Montessori data, a significant experimental study illustrates the importance of play for teaching preschool children to regulate their own behavior so that they can profit from classroom instruction.[58] Measured as early as 3 to 5 years of age, three core abilities collectively referred to as *cognitive control* predict reading and math achievement from kindergarten through high school.[59] These abilities are (1) inhibition, (2) holding and operating on information in working memory, and (3) flexibly adjusting attention to changes in task requirements. In addition, poor cognitive control skills link to emotional and behavior problems.

In the Tools of the Mind (Tools) curriculum, inspired by Vygotsky's theory,[60] scaffolding of cognitive control is woven into virtually all classroom activities. For example, teachers encourage complex make-believe play, guiding children in jointly planning play scenarios before enacting them. Teachers also lead rule-switching games in which regular movement patterns shift often, requiring flexibility of attention. Diamond, Barnett, Thomas, and Munro randomly assigned 150 children to Tools classrooms or to comparison classrooms with similar content and activities, but without addressing the issue of cognitive control.[61] Importantly, low-income children often have limited cognitive control. At the end of their preschool experience, children were given two cognitive-control measures. Children from Tools classrooms showed significantly greater ability to switch attention and to engage in response inhibition—important executive function behaviors—compared with children from the comparison classrooms. In fact, the children in the Tools classrooms seemed so far ahead that the experiment was halted so that the control children could receive the Tools curriculum as well. Importantly, the more rigorous tests of executive function correlated significantly with the Tools children's scores on standardized academic measures. The authors concluded:

> Although play is often thought frivolous, it may be essential. Tools uses mature dramatic play to help improve executive functions. Yet preschools are under pressure to limit play.[61]

THE EVIDENCE: PART 1—PLAYFUL LEARNING PROMOTES ACADEMIC GAIN

Language and Literacy

Literacy rests on an oral language foundation.[62] Outside of the family, play among peers serves as the crucible for the oral language skills that children need to engage in reading.[63] As Bruner suggested,[64] "the most complicated grammatical and pragmatic forms of language appear first in play activity."[65] An extensive research literature suggests that a whole-child approach emphasizing active learning through play stimulates both cognitive and social development. This literature suggests that children benefit from both unstructured play and more structured teacher-guided play. Importantly, data to support the claim that children learn best from playful, guided interactions can be adduced in the areas of language and literacy, numeracy, attention, and problem solving. Also critical is that under guided play, teachers are goal oriented but sensitive and responsive to the children's behaviors.

Galda reported that preschoolers engaged in much commentary about language when creating make-believe scenes, even using complex mental-state verbs such as *say, talk, tell, write,* and *explain.*[66] Dickinson and Moreton echoed this finding, noting that the amount of time 3-year-olds spent talking with peers while pretending was positively associated with the size of their vocabularies two years later after they had begun kindergarten.[67]

The advanced language capabilities that emerge in play with peers offer not only a window into children's growing competencies but also a link to literacy. In the *Home School Study of Language and Literacy Development,* Dickinson and Tabors followed 74 children from low-income homes from 3 years of age through middle school.[68] The researchers found clear and consistent relationships between children's talk during play and their later literacy outcomes. The conversations children had during the course of the preschool day—especially those that occurred during free play—were related to a broad range of skills in oral language and print at the end of kindergarten. A singular focus on print, Dickinson concluded, is clearly to the "detriment" of children who need the rich language exchanges that occur during play. "Free play is the time when children flex their linguistic and conceptual muscles and contribute to each other's development."[69] Play occurs when children encounter much new vocabulary and engage in extended discourse. Indeed, after reviewing 20 studies on literacy and play, Roskos and Christie concluded that play boosts literacy by "serving as a language experience that can build connections between oral and written modes of expression."[70] In this light, it is interesting that when children lose play time to television viewing, their vocabulary is worse.

In one longitudinal investigation, Bergen and Mauer found that 4-year-olds' play (in the form of rhyming games, making shopping lists, and "reading" story books to stuffed animals) predicted both language and reading readiness (including phonological awareness—that words are made of smaller units) after the children had entered kindergarten.[71] Kindergartners with increased phonological awareness relative to their peers, in turn, had more diverse vocabularies, used more complex sentences, and showed the extent of their competencies most often in playful environments. They also were less likely than classmates scoring low in phonological awareness to have reading difficulties in first grade. A host of studies by Christie led to the same conclusion:[72] Children demonstrate their most advanced language skills in playful environments, and these language skills are strongly related to literacy development.[73]

Finally, Neuman and Roskos reported that words embedded in playful contexts are learned better and faster.[74] When given the opportunity, young children eagerly incorporate literacy props into their dramatic play and engage in increased amounts of narrative, emergent reading and writing[75]—all skills that they need to learn to read. Thus, correlational research overwhelmingly suggests that play among peers fosters prereading skills by encouraging symbol manipulation (both linguistic and in the form of props) and attention to language qua language (as in rhyming games).

Research also demonstrates that playful learning with adults contributes to the acquisition of literacy skills. Bellin and Singer conducted an experimental study called *My Magic Story Car* using low-income children and adults.[76] Using five imaginative games seen on DVDs (e.g., the Lost Puppy Game), children "drove" their cars (cardboard boxes) to play the games. Each game targeted different literacy skills, such as rhyming, print knowledge, alphabet letters, phonological awareness, compound words, emergent writing, vocabulary, and facts about books (e.g., that books have titles, covers, and authors; are read from left to right). Adults were given the materials as well as a printed manual to use with small groups of 4-year-olds over a 2-week period in this random-assignment study.

A comparison of pretest and posttest knowledge revealed that the experimental play group made significant gains over no-intervention controls in key emergent literacy skills (e.g., phonological awareness and print knowledge). Children even incorporated the skills they learned in the games into their daily activities. This research is among many studies that boast a relationship between guided play and reading readiness.[77]

After reviewing 12 studies on literacy and play, Roskos and Christie concluded that "play provides settings that promote literacy activity, skills, and strategies . . . and can provide opportunities to teach and learn literacy."[78] This is not to suggest, however, that researchers understand the mechanisms behind these effects. Although Roskos and Christie find evidence for a clear relationship between play and literacy, they urge researchers to define both constructs more carefully and to conduct more experimental research that establishes causal links between play and literacy skills. Johnson, Christie, and Wardle also call for follow-up studies of the results of literacy play interventions and for the uncovering of "sleeper effects"[79]—delayed benefits of learning through play. Despite the fact that more work needs to be done, substantial evidence from observational, longitudinal, and even experimental studies suggests that play and guided playful learning with adult supervision can support both the continued development of language and the acquisition of emergent literacy skills.

Numeracy and Spatial Concepts

Cognitive effects of play are just as far reaching in terms of the development of numeracy. For example, in their book, *Knowledge Under Construction,* Daniel Ness and Stephen J. Farenga speak of learning about space by thinking about "castles in the air."[80] They represent this concept through concrete manipulations of playthings. Their book demonstrates that children learn about space, geometry, and even architecture as they play with a simple logs, tracks, blocks, and Legos.

Ginsburg concurs, noting that play often stimulates "early math" in young children's everyday experiences as children experiment with shape, space, measurement, and magnitude.[81] Seo and Ginsburg videotaped 90 four-year-old and five-year-old children during free play (including sociodramatic play and make-believe) in their preschools for 15-minute segments.[82] Regardless of children's social class, three categories of mathematical activity were widely prevalent. The first is pattern and shape play (exploration of patterns and spatial forms), which occurred in an average of 21% of segments; the second is magnitude (statement of magnitude or comparison of two or more items to evaluate relative magnitude), which occurred in about 13% of the segments; and the third is enumeration (numerical judgment or quantification), which occurred in about 12% of the segments. Taken together, these results suggest that during fully 46% of the 15-minute segments, children's natural play contains the roots of mathematical learning. In play, children also frequently use spatial relations and measurement (tallest and shortest).[83] Block play and play with construction toys stimulate these mathematically and spatially relevant competencies. Using play as a guide, teachers can find out what children already know and can build on their burgeoning knowledge.

An ongoing study in our laboratory further supports the importance of play—especially guided play—for children's exposure to spatial and numerical language. Preschool children and their parents were randomly assigned to one of three conditions. In the *free play* condition, children and their parents were given a set of blocks and simply told to play as they liked. In the *guided play* condition, they were given the same blocks but offered a picture of a structure that they were to build together. In the *preassembled structure* condition, they were given the blocks and an already assembled structure and were told to play as they liked. The dependent variable in this phase of the study was how much spatial language parents used when they interacted with their child. Sentences such as, "The red block goes on the green one" and "Use the big one first" occurred more frequently in the guided play condition than in the other two conditions.

Results suggested that the structure of a play context influences the nature of the play interaction that takes place. Parents in the guided play condition produced significantly more spatial language than parents who had been in the free play or preassembled conditions. In Phase II of the study, all child-parent pairs were in a guided play condition given a picture of a new structure to build together. They produced an equivalent amount of spatial language—using spatial terms, on average, in one of every 12 words. Children learn spatial concepts by hearing them used naturally in conversation. This study indicates that while parents guide play, they provide crucial information about the meaning and use of spatial concepts.[84]

Other studies also have demonstrated the power of guided play and playful learning for spatial outcomes in older children. By way of example, children's success on spatial tests increased in experimental studies in which the children used small blocks to duplicate designs and played certain video games that actively engaged them. The games required the children to respond quickly and to mentally rotate visual images.[85] Correlational evidence suggests that children who participate in manipulative activities, such as block play, model building, and carpentry, do better on spatial tasks.[86]

Research has found that developmentally appropriate play and guided play offer rich contexts for children's learning, possibly because they engage children. Playing children are motivated children. One excellent example comes from Gelman, who found that children even as young as 2.5 and 3 years understand the "cardinal counting principle"—that the last number counted in a set is the amount the set contains.[87] This knowledge, however, is only shown when children engage in a playful task in which they are asked to predict the number of items and then count them. When they are asked to count, for no specific purpose, in a laboratory task, young children do not appear to be competent. Although it is still not clear why children cannot succeed in count-alone counting tasks, Gelman concluded that children reveal what they know in the classroom when mathematical tasks are embedded in games, "where children enjoy and readily engage in the activities."[88] Preschoolers learn and display their knowledge of math best in playful environments.

Another example comes from recent experimental research by Ramani and Siegler, who demonstrated that 124 five-year-old, low-income children who played a linear board game such as "Chutes and Ladders" outperformed their peers on four diverse mathematical tasks: numerical magnitude, number line estimation, counting, and numeral identification.[89] Remarkably, this difference appeared with only four 15- to 20-minute sessions within a 2-week period and lasted for up to 9 weeks. The control group played a color game for the same amount of time and failed to show these gains. Thus, content-directed playful learning can have dramatic effects on mathematical understanding.

In a recent statement on young children's mathematics education (where mathematical concepts include spatial tasks such as pattern matching and shape knowledge), Ginsburg, Lee, and Boyd underscore that mathematical education in preschool should include both play and a more organized curriculum.[90] However, even the more organized or formal teaching should capitalize on playful engaged learning. This statement speaks to helping teachers identify teachable moments that involve, "careful observation of play . . . that can be exploited to promote learning."[91] The report also reviews successful curricula that use developmentally appropriate and playful material, "designed to help children extend and mathematicize their daily activities, from building blocks . . . to art and stories . . ."[92] As in language and literacy, both free play and guided playful learning are central to optimal preschool spatial learning.

The Role of Play in Attention and Problem Solving

Play builds cognitive knowledge by offering countless opportunities for sustained attention,[93] problem solving, symbolic representation (e.g., the banana as a phone),[94] memory development,[95] and hypothesis testing.[96] Indeed, the play-based Tools of the Mind curriculum, expressly aimed at modifying children's executive function, succeeded in improving lower-income children's attentional focus and academic achievement.[97]

With respect to problem solving, children use play to disentangle ambiguities they find in the world and to test their incipient hypotheses about how things work.[98] One illustrative study by Smith and Dutton experimentally evaluated the relative impact of play experiences versus explicit tutelage on problem solving in 4-year-olds.[99] Researchers asked the children to retrieve a marble from a box that they could see through a transparent door. The children could solve the problem only by assembling sticks using two small blocks with holes. Children in the experimental and control groups had a brief period to manipulate sticks of varying lengths and play with the blocks.

There were two experimental groups. Children in the play condition continued playing with the sticks and blocks, whereas those in the training condition watched an adult demonstrate how to join the sticks together and were asked to copy her actions. The two control groups each proceeded directly to one of two problem-solving tasks. Both sets of experimental children solved the first problem (which required combining two sticks) more rapidly and with fewer hints than the control children. On the second problem (which required combining three sticks, thus, more innovative use of the materials), children in the play group outperformed all other groups, taking less than half as much time to find the solution, requiring fewer hints, and appearing more motivated.

In short, play and playful learning are linked to school readiness for language, literacy, and numeracy. Furthermore, executive processes such as attention and problem solving are buttressed in play and in more formal playful curricula.[100] The association between play and cognitive outcomes emerges in studies where adults provide instruction in a playful manner and where children explore solutions to problems in free play. Playful learning seems to capture children's attention and to offer the opportunities for both knowledge acquisition and flexible experimentation. These results appear in both correlational and experimental studies.

THE EVIDENCE: PART 2—PLAY ADVANCES SOCIAL DEVELOPMENT

As Raver concluded, "From the last two decades of research, it is unequivocally clear that children's emotional and behavioral adjustment is important for their chances of early school success."[101] Play helps children learn to subordinate desires to social rules, cooperate with others willingly, and engage in socially appropriate behavior— all skills vital to adjusting well to the demands of school. Make-believe play has been found to be crucial for building children's social competence, including their ability to self-regulate and cope emotionally.

Vygotsky suggested that in play, children recreate roles and situations that reflect their sociocultural world.[102] As with language use (see above), at first these competencies are more advanced in play than in other contexts, and they gradually transfer to children's everyday behavior. Research supports Vygotsky's claim: "In play it is as though [the child] were a head taller than himself . . .".[103] Play is important for building social competence and confidence in dealing with peers.[104] It is also central to self-regulation, or children's ability to manage their own behavior and emotions. In play, children practice these skills.[105]

Children often use play as a means for coping with distress. An experimental study by Barnett and Storm illustrates the role of play in regulating intense, negative emotion.[106] Researchers exposed preschoolers either to a stressful movie scene (Lassie became separated from her master in a storm) or to the stressful movie scene plus a positive resolution (Lassie and her master were reunited). Children then had a free-play period after the film. Initial anxiety levels of the two groups, based on a physiological measure (palm sweating) and a self-report (choosing a picture of a face showing emotion that represented how the child felt) were comparable, but anxiety in the stressful movie group increased following viewing. However, anxiety declined sharply in children in the stressful movie group after the play period, during which those children spent more time enacting events related to the Lassie scene than did control children.

In another experimental study, 74 three-year-olds were observed as they exhibited distress at the departure of their mother on the first day of preschool.[107] High- and low-anxious children, distinguished on the basis of observations (clinging, pleading, crying) and physiological reaction (palm sweating), participated in either a free-play or a story-reading session. Relative to the other children, high-anxious children in the free-play session engaged in more play thematically directed at resolving conflict, and showed a greater decline in physiological anxiety. The Barnett studies are not alone in showing that the stress of transitions is eased when preschool children have the opportunity to engage in play.[108]

Furthermore, research confirms that make-believe play contributes to emotional understanding, which helps children get along with others. Children have many opportunities in play to consider the causes, consequences, and behavioral signs of emotion.[109] During sociodramatic play, preschoolers engage in especially frequent acting out of feelings and "emotion talk" with siblings and friends.[110] Knowledge about emotions, in turn, predicts friendly, considerate behavior; willingness to make amends after harming another; and peer acceptance as early as 3 to 5 years of age.[111] This holds for middle-income children as well as for inner-city poor African-American and Hispanic children.[112]

Dramatic play is also related to self-regulatory behaviors. Elias and Berk, for example, in a short-term longitudinal study, observed 51 middle-income 3- and 4-year-olds in their preschool classrooms during the fall (Time 1) and the spring (Time 2).[113] During the fall, each child's play in the block and housekeeping areas was observed for four 10-minute periods, each on a separate day, with time-sampling codes assessing the quantity and maturity of make-believe, based on the Smilansky scale.[114] In addition, during both seasons, observers rated children's behavior for self-regulatory maturity during four cleanup and four circle-time periods.

Results were consistent with the contribution of make-believe to future self-regulation. Controlling for verbal ability and fall self-regulation scores, time spent in complex sociodramatic play (involving three of the following play elements—adoption of a social role, verbal dialogue for pretend characters, nonreplica substitute objects, or verbal descriptions substituted for objects and situations) was positively correlated with spring cleanup performance. Similar results were not obtained for circle time; in this totally adult-directed activity, teachers regulated children's behavior, thereby making it difficult to assess children's self-regulation variations.

For children who have difficult life circumstances, emotional problems, or developmental delays, play may be even more critical. Haight, Black, Jacobsen, and Sheridan demonstrated how children who have been traumatized can use pretend play with their mothers to work through the effects of stress.[115] Relatedly, children with autism have a limited ability to engage in symbolic play. Research has suggested that creating interventions that are based in play holds promise for helping these children overcome some of their social limitations.[116]

INTERVENTION STUDIES: TRAINING CHILDREN TO PLAY

Along with some experimental data, most of the studies reviewed thus far report correlations between play behavior (free and guided) and various social outcomes. Of course, correlations can have many sources. Intervention studies that train children to play support the claim that play facilitates the development of various skills—social, cognitive, and academic.

Several training studies using experimental and control groups taught children to engage in fantasy or sociodramatic play and then assessed cognitive and social outcomes. The classic study was conducted by Smilansky in Israel with low-income North African and Middle Eastern immigrant children.[117] Smilansky posited that enhancing children's sociodramatic play might have an impact on their language performance. Play training administered by the children's teachers led to an increase in the quality and amount of children's sociodramatic play as well as to gains in verbal fluency, mean length of utterance, richer vocabulary, and greater language comprehension. Smilansky suggested that play is essential for success in school:

> Problem solving in most school subjects requires a great deal of make-believe: visualizing how the Eskimos live, reading stories, imagining a story and writing it down, solving arithmetic problems, and determining what will come next. History, geography, and literature are all make-believe. All of these are conceptual constructions that are never directly experienced by the child.[118]

Although Smilansky's research was groundbreaking, it did not evaluate the data statistically and could not isolate the cause of the beneficial effects of sociodramatic play. Smilansky did not correlate the amount of time children spent in make-believe with their academic success.

Subsequent training studies that built on Smilansky's observations were more methodologically sophisticated. Saltz and Johnson trained disadvantaged preschoolers to enact familiar fairy tales, trading roles from session to session over 6-month period.[119] They found large effects on standardized intelligence measures of story interpretation, sequential memory, and empathy in comparison to no-intervention control groups. In an attempt to isolate the source of these cognitive effects, and especially to evaluate whether their results were simply the result of the verbal stimulation offered by the adults during fantasy play, Saltz, Dixon, and Johnson included three experimental groups in their next study.[120] One group was trained as before to enact fairy tales (thematic fantasy play), a second was trained to enact realistic experiences such as going to the doctor (sociodramatic play), and a third group heard and discussed the fairy tales with an adult but did not enact them (fantasy discussion). Finally, a no-treatment control group received no training but engaged in typical preschool activities (e.g., cutting and pasting).

If verbal stimulation was the source of the effect in the Saltz, Dixon, and Johnson study, the three experimental groups should show roughly equivalent effects. Results suggest that, "verbal stimulation *by itself* cannot have produced the effects found in this experiment" because the fantasy discussion condition had at least as much verbal stimulation as the thematic fantasy play group and yet tested no differently than the control children.[121] Yet, relative to the children in the other groups, children in the thematic fantasy playgroup manifested significant gains in intellectual performance on standardized IQ tests and on interpreting sequential events, distinguishing reality from fantasy, delaying impulsive behavior, and empathizing with others. These effects occurred over and above the effects of hearing stories or even of acting out realistic events.

Dansky reported similar findings.[122] Economically disadvantaged preschoolers were either trained in sociodramatic play or in exploratory (nonfantasy) play. According to teacher report, sociodramatic play training led to more spontaneous make-believe, role play, and social interaction, and more imaginativeness. Importantly, training children in sociodramatic play also led to greater improvements on cognitive tasks, including verbal comprehension, story sequencing, creativity, and causal reasoning.

Taken together, the data studying the advantages of fantasy play from both observational and intervention studies are, as Kagan and Lowenstein argue, "irrefutable."[123] Play, in the form of make-believe fantasy play or sociodramatic play, fosters children's development, expanding both cognitive and social skills. Fantasy play advances both cognitive and social growth for four reasons. First, it allows adults a view of children's highest level of skill, providing teachers with a clearer look at what children can do. Second, it enables children to practice the lessons of the day (whether cognitive or emotional) in a safe and relatively unrestricted way. Third, it offers a connected and meaningful symbolic narrative that encourages children to distinguish the real from the fantasy, to consider other points of view, and to work out social understandings. Fourth, playful exchanges motivate and engage children. Research abounds suggesting that children are more apt to learn when they are interested and engaged in the material they are learning.[124] Bredekamp comments on the relationship of play to learning the ABCs:

> Preschool children are highly motivated to engage in pretend play. Play is such a pleasurable activity for young children, in fact, that there is no need to coerce or cajole them to participate as there often is in other types of teacher-directed activity.[125]

DIRECT INSTRUCTION COMPARED WITH ACTIVE, DEVELOPMENTALLY APPROPRIATE LEARNING

As noted above, discussions about the value of playful learning are at the heart of debates between direct-instruction and developmentally appropriate approaches. Direct-instruction models are more teacher-directed, learning is more compartmentalized (e.g., specific slots in the day are allocated for math or reading) and students are generally more passive, working to meet a set of unified standards. Teachers in this model are less likely to adapt to the interest or needs of the child. In contrast, developmentally appropriate schools are aligned with a Piagetian constructivist or a Vygotskian social-constructivist approach, in which learning is integrated across subject areas and conveyed in meaningful ways related to children's everyday experiences (e.g., a birthday party requires a child to both count and write invitations) and in which "children are active agents who reflect on and coordinate their own thoughts, rather than *merely* absorbing those of others."[126]

Studies have compared children in "academic" preschool and kindergarten classrooms that emphasize direct, formal instruction[127] with children who are in developmentally appropriate classrooms in which play is a central means of learning.[128] Dependent variables in these studies (both concurrent and longitudinal) fall into three categories: measures of children's motivation, academic achievement (e.g., in reading or math), and social and emotional adjustment to school, including measures of stress and prosocial behavior.

A review of the literature by Hart, Burts, and Charlesworth[129] revealed that enrollment in less developmentally appropriate classrooms (i.e., classrooms where direct-instructional practices are used) was associated with more child stress[130] and with less positive academic outcomes at the end of the school year[131] than did their peers in developmentally appropriate classrooms. In addition, children in direct-instruction classrooms had worse behavioral outcomes[132] and worse motivational outcomes.[133]

Academic Comparisons

At best, only a short-term advantage in academic outcomes is associated with direct-instruction approaches or with approaches that focus on literacy and mathematical knowledge per se.[134] Datta, McHalle, and Mitchell examined 6,000 children at 37 Head Start sites on a range of academic variables. Although direct instruction seemed to endow children with academic gains, these gains were not long-lived. A debate on the ability of the direct-instruction model to raise children's achievement continues to rage.[135]

In the cognitive realm, Bryant, Burchinal, Lau, and Sparling[136] found a correlation between children's home environment using the HOME scale that measures items available in children's homes[137] and children's ability to profit from classrooms with developmentally appropriate practices versus direct instruction. The 145 Head Start children studied were between 3 and 5 years of age. Results indicated that those in classrooms with developmentally appropriate practices performed better on measures of achievement and preacademic skills than did those in direct-instruction classrooms.

Marcon assessed the differential effects of academically focused versus developmentally appropriate kindergartens on a range of developmental domains and early skill acquisition in two cohorts of poor inner-city kindergartners (n = 307).[138] Marcon found a detrimental impact of the overly academic kindergarten on boys' development and school achievement. Although girls were found to be developmentally more ready for academic experiences, they ironically achieved greater mastery of basic skills when enrolled in developmentally appropriate kindergartens.

Assel, Landry, Swank, and Gunnewig evaluated two curricular approaches (Let's Begin with the Letter People, and Doors to Discovery) to the teaching of reading and language across three different preschool environments (Head Start, Title I, universal preschool, and a control group) in a random assignment study.[139] The two curricular models included playful learning about letters, vocabulary, and rhyming. The control classrooms used no particular prereading curricula but an amalgamation of worksheets and "outdated curricula" that focused on elements of literacy and language noted in the state standards. Results suggested that children who experienced the two playful curricula outperformed children in the control group. As the authors noted in commenting on those curricula, "Both avoided didactic, highly structured approaches, but rather emphasized children learning in meaningful contexts in highly engaging 'hands-on' activities."[140]

The research seems to suggest that although spontaneous play supports children's construction of foundations for mathematics and literacy, curricula that capitalize on children's need to learn in a playful manner bring children to higher levels of achievement than do purely didactic curricula.

Socioemotional and Motivational Comparisons

Hart et al. used a quasi-experimental design to probe for concurrent relationships between classroom type and child stress behaviors.[141] The researchers identified classrooms that were more developmentally appropriate (emphasizing active experimentation and play) versus those that were less developmentally appropriate (emphasizing direct-instructional practices). The 102 preschoolers in the direct-instruction classrooms exhibited two times the level of stress behavior (based on classroom observations) seen in children in the developmentally appropriate preschool classrooms. In direct-instruction classrooms, children from low-income homes were significantly more stressed than children from middle-income homes, and males were more stressed than females, particularly during small-motor/paper-and-pencil activities.

Burts, Hart, Charlesworth, and Kirk compared kindergarten children on measures of stress behaviors (e.g., hand wringing, knee bouncing, attention getting, pencil tapping) in classrooms with developmentally appropriate (n = 20) versus direct-instructional practices (n = 17).[142] Children in the direct-instruction classroom exhibited significantly more stress behaviors than children in the developmentally appropriate classroom. Males exhibited marginally more overall stress behaviors than females.

In a subsequent study with more children, Burts et al. observed activities and stress behaviors of children in six developmentally appropriate (n = 111) and six direct-instruction (n = 113) kindergarten classrooms.[143] They replicated their prior finding that children in direct-instruction classrooms exhibited more overall stress than did children in developmentally appropriate classrooms. In particular, males in direct-instruction classrooms exhibited more stress than did males in developmentally appropriate classrooms. African Americans in direct-instruction classrooms exhibited more stress than Caucasians during transition, waiting, and teacher-directed whole-group activities, whereas Caucasians exhibited more stress during group story activities.

Results from the High Scope project also suggest that children in developmentally appropriate classrooms tend to surpass children in direct-instruction classrooms on social outcomes and that these effects are found regardless of children's economic class.[144]

Rescorla, Hyson, and Hirsh-Pasek examined both the social-emotional and academic progress of 94 children from 4 to 5 years of age as they moved from preschool to kindergarten.[145] These middle-class children attended preschools that were characterized as either direct-instruction or as developmentally appropriate, as judged by the *Classroom Practices Inventory*.[146] The *Classroom Practices Inventory* is based on criteria from the National Association for the Education of Young Children guidelines, which observes classrooms for characteristics such as "Teachers expect children to respond correctly with one right answer" (direct instruction) or "Teachers ask questions which encourage children to give more than one right answer" (developmentally appropriate). Importantly, this classroom observational rating also probed for dramatic play, a practice found to be more prevalent in the classrooms that displayed other developmentally appropriate characteristics. Using preschool classroom type as one predictor, child outcomes were examined in academics,[147] creativity,[148] and emotional well-being.[149] Results suggested that by 5 years of age, children in both the academically and more socially oriented classrooms performed similarly. That is, there was no academic advantage to learning numbers and letters early for middle-class children. Those attending more direct-instruction classrooms with less emphasis on play, however, were less creative, slightly more anxious, and less positive about school.[150]

Similar results were obtained in an experimental study conducted by Stipek, Feiler, Daniels, and Milburn.[151] The children studied were 227 poor minority children as well as middle-class 4- to 6-year-olds. The researchers compared achievement and motivational variables in children who attended either developmentally appropriate or direct-instruction preschools and kindergartens.

With respect to behavioral and motivational variables, children enrolled in direct-instruction classrooms had relatively negative outcomes. Compared with children in developmentally appropriate classrooms, children from academic classrooms rated their own abilities significantly lower, had lower expectations for success on academic tasks, showed more dependency on adults for permission and approval, showed less pride in their accomplishments, and claimed to worry more about school. These results were the same for low- and middle-income children and for preschoolers and kindergartners. The significance of these finding should not be underestimated. Once children begin to perceive themselves as relatively less able to profit from classroom instruction than their peers, those perceptions have long-term effects on children's self-esteem and feelings about school.[152]

These studies are but a sample of those that compared children's achievement and socioemotional adjustment in developmentally appropriate and direct-instruction classrooms. One potential shortcoming of these studies is that most are concurrent and thus limited to documenting relatively short-term effects. The next set of studies uses longitudinal data for a more extended look at the effects of these two types of classroom environments.

Longitudinal Studies

A study by Stipek, Feiler, Byler, Ryan, Milburn, and Salmon resulted in outcomes similar to those just reported. They assessed the children on cognitive competencies and motivation at the beginning and end of the preschool or kindergarten year and then again at the end of the next year (kindergarten or first grade). Stipek et al. reported that preschoolers and kindergartners in classrooms that emphasized basic skills scored lower on achievement tests (reading and math) and on six subscales from the short form of the McCarthy Scales of Children's Abilities than did children in developmentally appropriate programs.[153] These negative effects were also apparent one year later, at the end of kindergarten and first grade, respectively. On motivational variables such as perceptions of competence, attitudes toward school, anxiety, affect, risk taking, expectations for success, independence, and persistence, outcomes were significantly worse for children in the preschool programs emphasizing basic skills using structured, teacher-directed approaches that created a relatively negative social climate. Kindergarten results were more mixed.

Longitudinal follow-ups to the research by Stipek et al. reviewed above indicate that direct-instructional practices are particularly negative for preschoolers, undermining

both motivation and cognitive competencies.[154] Even beyond preschool and kindergarten, the data continue to
make the case for the advantages of developmentally appropriate practices over direct instruction in both academic and cognitive outcomes.

For example, Frede and Barnett examined the impact of developmentally appropriate public preschools on
disadvantaged children's skills in first grade.[155] The researchers found that large-scale public-school programs
can provide developmentally appropriate experiences
for disadvantaged young children that contribute to increased skills in first grade (e.g., High Scope). Long-term
results compared children in the High Scope program
with those attending playful nursery programs or with
those children in schools with direct instruction. There
were some positive short-term gains in IQ for the direct-
instruction group in kindergarten. In the long run, however, the direct-instruction kindergartners had seven
times as many emotional problems and were four times
more likely to be arrested by the age of 23.[156]

Hart, Yang, Charlesworth, and Burt also conducted a
longitudinal study that compared children who received
direct instruction with those who received developmentally appropriate practices.[157] Results showed that from
kindergarten through the third grade, children receiving
direct instruction experienced more stress than did the
other group. Furthermore, stress predicted the appear-
ance of hyperactive and distractible behaviors as well as
greater hostility and aggression. These findings emerged
across gender, race, and socioeconomic status.

Finally, findings from the Cost Quality Study add to
the advantage of play-based developmentally appropriate
pedagogy over a direct-instruction pedagogy when they
looked at teacher-directed versus more child-directed approaches to learning.[158] With a large subject base of 826
children from kindergarten to second grade, the Cost
Quality Study used a stratified random sample design to

ask how the quality of child care in preschool affected child outcomes up to second grade. As part of this study, Howes and Byler (unpublished data) found that children experiencing developmentally appropriate pedagogy in kindergarten had higher levels of academic achievement and scored higher in receptive language as well as in mathematics and reading in second grade.[159]

Note that the studies reviewed above find some gains from direct instruction. Children who experience direct instruction with emphasis on drill-and-practice achieved gains in general cognition[160] and literacy,[161] but few gains in numeracy.[162] Yet these gains are small compared with the gains achieved by children in programs that are more developmentally appropriate. Furthermore, the gains children achieved in "academic" classrooms appear to be short-lived and come at an emotional and motivational cost that can persist for years (e.g., High Scope).

PLAYFUL LEARNING: COMBINING THE BEST OF TEACHER-GUIDED AND DEVELOPMENTALLY APPROPRIATE PEDAGOGY

Much of the literature reviewed above treats direct instruction and developmentally appropriate approaches as mutually exclusive. But increasingly, the programs that offer the best traction for children's achievement and socioemotional growth take a hybrid approach. That is, within developmentally appropriate education, *there is room for real instruction that is playful.* Play and learning are not incompatible. Children can and should learn content, whether mathematics, language, or pre-literacy, in socially rich and meaningful contexts rather than in didactic environments that are not engaging or responsive.

Some examples of broad-based curricular initiatives illustrate this point. Researchers studying Montessori's and Tools of the Mind's curricula (discussed above) conducted random assignment studies on these curricula's effects. In unique ways, these programs emphasize goal-directed activities where teachers encourage children to participate in playful activities that heighten their involvement and attentional focus. Importantly, these programs differ from traditional direct-instruction curricula because, although they offer teacher guidance, they are encouraging and responsive to students. Academic and social outcomes that emerge from these programs indicate that children profit from playful learning approaches. Even more focused programs that concentrate on a particular curricular area such as reading or mathematics demonstrate the benefits children gain from approaches that unite play and teacher-guided playful learning.[163]

A CALL FOR DEVELOPMENTALLY
APPROPRIATE PRESCHOOL PEDAGOGY

Universal preschool has already been implemented in states such as California, Oklahoma, New York, Florida, and New Jersey.[164] It is on the near horizon for many other states. Economists such as Heckman and Masterov have suggested that for every dollar invested in high-quality preschool education for children from disadvantaged backgrounds, society reaps $3.78 to $10.15 in return.[165] In part, this prompted the move toward universal preschools. The national dialogue, then, no longer asks *whether* society should educate young children, but *how*.

Psychologists have much to add to this conversation. As Kagan and Lowenstein have written, "The literature is clear: Diverse strategies that combine play and more structured efforts are effective accelerators of children's readiness for school and long-term development."[166] The pendulum has swung too far in the direction of *all work and no play*. It is imperative that we offer a corrective by reinserting play and playful learning back into preschool pedagogy.

The literature reviewed in this text speaks to multiple ways in which diverse play experiences benefit young children. Observational, longitudinal, and experimental (including play training) studies all find that playful learning predicts both academic and social development. The advantages of playful learning experiences are seen across economic and ethnic boundaries. Furthermore, those educational environments that embrace playful learning characteristics better engage children, who become more school ready. Developmentally appropriate programs include opportunities for children to engage in both exploratory dramatic play and teacher-guided play. Thus, both child-initiated and teacher- (or adult-) guided play seem to offer academic and social benefits for young children. The best preschool programs are those that permit some free play but are not limited to free play. The best programs also meld free play with adult-guided instruction in playful ways, as was seen in the newer models such as Tools of the Mind.

Although the weight of the evidence supports play as a central ingredient for preschool pedagogy, the research to date does have its limitations. Throughout our review, the use of the terms *playful learning* and *play* remain quite general. How does one determine whether a reading program, for example, is work or play? Does practicing the alphabet by worksheet relegate it to direct instruction, whereas a more child-initiated alphabet song would be more playful? In part, the definitional problem has haunted play research since its inception. Perhaps it is more profitable to think about play and work not as diametrically opposed categorical constructs but rather as constructs on a continuum anchored by teacher-produced worksheets on the one end and by children's open and exploratory play on the other. Playful learning guided by a teacher with learning objectives falls in the middle of the continuum. With playful learning, children are not searching for one right answer or wandering freely about the classroom without supervision. Rather, children feel free to explore while the teacher makes sure that they encounter certain content. The evidence presented above suggests that successful preschool programs are characterized by this kind of guided play.

With a clearer operational definition of playful learning, we could isolate the mechanisms through which play influences children's learning. That is, we know that play fosters academic and social learning. We also know that play is characteristic of developmentally appropriate pedagogy. Yet, many of the studies do not directly examine the pathways through which playful learning relates to child outcomes.

We need more longitudinal data to support the building consensus that playful learning and guided play advance academic and social learning in preschool and buffer children's transition to formal school. Furthermore, newer research such as that emanating from the Tools of the Mind program offer direct—and experimental—findings on this issue. More research in this area is sorely needed, as is research on individual differences in frequencies and types of play, and how these differences relate to later academic and social success.

The data mandate that both free play and playful learning should command a central role in high-quality education for preschoolers. Children taught in a more playful manner almost always achieve more than children who are subjected to more direct teaching methods. Furthermore, the data show that academic programs that emphasize more direct instruction have unintended social and emotional consequences, creating students who are less likely to get along with their peers and feel comfortable in school, and more likely to show evidence of stress-induced hyperactivity, to be hostile, and to engage in antisocial acts.[167]

The best preschool education is one that embraces the whole child, is playful and rich in opportunities for exploration and meaning-making, and is under adult guidance. Years of evidence paint a picture of a balanced school environment in which children can and do *learn to play* and *play to learn*. Despite the wealth of scientific data, the benefits of playful environments for young children are often downplayed in the design of early education curricula. Indeed, the lack of adequate play time for children prompted a recent report from the American Academy of Pediatrics that concluded:

> Multiple forces are interacting to effectively reduce many children's ability to reap the benefits of play. As we strive to create the optimal developmental milieu for children, it remains imperative that play is included along with academic and social enrichment opportunities.[168]

The emphasis on narrowly defined learning, as promoted by the current climate of high-stakes testing and accountability, relegates play to the status of an extraneous embellishment. It treats preschoolers as if they are miniature primary school children and as if all that matters are the child's cognitive skills. [169] It is time to define educational goals in a way that respects what research has found about the value of play and playful learning. Play is the furthest thing from a waste of children's time; it should return it to its rightful place in the curriculum.

As Sternberg[170] suggested when referring to primary school curricula, "Ironically, the skills we value most of all in the conventional school curriculum seem to be those that often matter least in life." We could not agree more.

THREE

Epilogue

In March of 2007, a distinguished group of scholars gathered in Santiago, Chile. Together with teachers and policy makers, they asked how recent developments in cognition, brain science, and child psychology could inform decisions about how to best educate the next generation. By the close of the conference, several things were clear to both the researchers and the practitioners. First, brain science, with its rapidly advancing data, holds exciting promise for education that is yet to be fully realized.[1] Researchers are only beginning to understand how the teaching of reading, math, or social skills can be informed by brain data.[2] Indeed, the first journal linking brain and education, *Mind, Brain, and Education,* appeared under Kurt Fisher's editorship during the same month as the Chilean conference.

Second, the researchers noted that substantive data from decades of research in child development are *directly* relevant to how children learn. Curricula for young children should be based on the accumulated scientific knowledge. The seven principles below are largely derived from those presented in what is now called the Santiago Declaration.[3] Not coincidentally, the principles below are completely in accord with the literature that has been reviewed in this monograph and are optimized in curricula that include an emphasis on playful learning. Many books provide an empirical foundation for these principles—books that are classics in science and policy—such as *Neurons to Neighborhoods;*[4] the highly acclaimed National Research Council books, *Eager to Learn*[5] and *How People Learn;*[6] Laura Berk's *Awakening Children's Minds: How Parents and Teachers Can Make a Difference;*[7] Zigler, Singer, and Bishop-Josef's book, *Children's Play: Roots of Reading;*[8] and Hirsh-Pasek and Golinkoff's *Einstein Never Used Flashcards: How Our Children Really Learn and Why They Need to Play More and Memorize Less,*[9] among others.

HOW YOUNG CHILDREN LEARN: SEVEN PRINCIPLES

The evidence-based principles below have been used implicitly for years to guide the design of preschool educational curricula. However, the present movement toward creating preschool curricula in which there is no place for play, free or guided, is a form of "data blindness" that flies in the face of these learning principles. As Sawyer has argued, the accumulated data underpinning the science of learning, coupled with our knowledge of human development, has moved beyond the "instructionism" of the past where children's prior knowledge and dispositions to learn were essentially ignored.[10] Ignoring what children bring to the classroom in both the cognitive and social domains leads to bad pedagogy. Young learners need to understand how classroom instruction meshes with their own experiences. We know better how to deliver effective preschool instruction—and have for a long time. Our practices need to change to catch up with the knowledge base that is summarized in the seven principles below.

1. All policies, programs, and products directed toward young children should be sensitive to children's developmental age and ability as defined through research-based developmental trajectories. Developmental trajectories and milestones are better construed through ranges and patterns of growth rather than through absolute ages.

2. Children are active, not passive, learners, who acquire knowledge by examining and exploring their environment.

3. Children, like all humans, are fundamentally social beings who learn most effectively in socially sensitive and responsive environments via their interactions with caring adults and other children.

4. Children learn best when their social and emotional needs are met and when they learn life skills necessary for success. Self-regulation, flexibility and compromise, and the ability to take the perspective of the other are skills to be nurtured.

5. Young children learn most effectively when information is embedded in meaningful contexts that relate to their everyday lives rather than in artificial contexts that foster rote learning.

6. The *process* of learning is as important as the outcome. Facilitating children's language, attentional skills, problem solving, flexible thinking, and self-regulation is crucial to children's academic success and to accountability. Settings that promote these skills prepare confident, eager, engaged, and lifelong learners.

7. Recognizing that children have diverse skills and needs as well as different cultural and socioeconomic backgrounds encourages respect for individual differences and allows children to optimize their learning.

HOW PLAYFUL LEARNING ALIGNS WITH
THE MANDATE'S SEVEN PRINCIPLES OF LEARNING

In play, children are active explorers. In free and in dramatic play, children are the initiators of the experiences. In guided, playful learning, children are introduced to experiences that are full of content and reinforced with engaging pedagogy that supports learning. Playful learning is one of the strong characteristics of both the successful Tools of the Mind[11] and Montessori programs[12] reviewed in this text.

Playful learning also encourages sensitivity and responsiveness in *teachers*—characteristics that are hallmarks of high-quality programs.[13] Why is this so? First, playful learning is more likely to occur in environments that are philosophically more consistent with the *whole-child* as opposed to the *empty-vessel* caricatures of childhood. Environments that support the empty-vessel caricature need not be as sensitive to individual differences or to the perspective of the child. Second, playful environments are inherently less scripted and more flexible. When teachers take the child's perspective, they engage in what Hart and Risley called the social *dance* of learning, weaving back and forth to the child's tune as the child's learning advances.[14] Finally, teachers trained to consider the whole child and the importance of playful learning integrate the cognitive child with the social child, offering children opportunities to develop cooperation, self-regulation, and negotiation.[15] As Zigler bemoaned, the child is more than a brain.[16] When we attend to this fact in high-quality preschool programs, society experiences "a huge savings" as these children, "are less likely to become delinquent and criminal later on." In programs that emphasize playful learning, the child is treated as a whole child rather than as a set of loosely connected social, physical, or cognitive bins.

Playful learning also crosses content areas, nesting learning within broader and more meaningful contexts.

The work by Christie offers a prime example of children's heightened learning of vocabulary within the context of playful learning about tools and building.[17] Interestingly, children in playful contexts centered on tool use are not only learning about language but also about social collaboration and even about how many plastic nails it takes to attach a roof. The same can be said of the Bellin and Singer "My Magic Story Car" emergent literacy program.[18] Children interact in dyads in make-believe cars, submarines, or space ships that they create, going on imaginary trips where emergent literacy is essential.

There are two consequences of learning in more enriched and meaningful environments. First, children are more engaged in that learning, enjoying the process of acquiring new knowledge. Second and importantly, their knowledge is more entrenched and multiply reinforced—allowing children to use what they learn in more than one context. A main goal of education is *transfer:* taking information learned at school and flexibly applying it in new circumstances both inside and outside school walls. Although play-based education is currently under siege, the seven principles above, based in developmental and learning science, maximize children's ability to learn and transfer. In the book *How People Learn,* the authors comment:

> Many approaches to instruction look equivalent when the only measure of learning is memory for facts that were specifically presented. Instructional differences become more apparent when evaluated from the perspective of how well the learning transfers to new problems and settings.[19]

Ironically, because its mission is to improve education, the current culture around No Child Left Behind emphasizes memorization and scripted learning, and diminishing learning science research that supports transfer. If teachers are to teach children flexible and adaptive problem solving in the 21st century, schools must return to engaging and playful curricula.

PRESCHOOL EDUCATION FOR THE 21ST CENTURY

The seven principles offered above marry scientific findings with pedagogical implications. They go part of the way toward building a model for best practices in preschool education. But a preschool model based on playful learning might do even more than buttress outcomes on standardized tests of academic and social outcomes. It might also better prepare students to be lifelong learners who will eventually enter a world that is increasingly relying on global, socially sensitive and flexible thinkers. Appeals for a new generation of creative thinkers are now heard throughout the business world. In his 2005 best seller, *A Whole New Mind: Moving from the Information Age to the Conceptual Age,* Daniel Pink writes:

> The last few decades have belonged to a certain kind of person with a certain kind of mind—computer programmers who could crank code, lawyers who could craft contracts, MBAs who could crunch numbers. But the keys to the kingdom are changing hands. The future belongs to a very different kind of person with a very different kind of mind—creators and empathizers, pattern recognizers, and meaning makers. These people—artists, inventors, designers, storytellers, caregivers, consolers, big picture thinkers—will now reap society's richest rewards and share its greatest joys.[20]

One of Pink's central messages is that we need more creative thinking in business. Play inspires the kind of thinking that best prepares children for the demands of the global workplace.

The same message is trumpeted by author Elizabeth Edersheim in her book, *The Definitive Drucker.*[21] Heralded as one of the top business books in 2007, this book speaks to the emerging face of business in the 21st century. Based on interviews with Peter Drucker, the father of modern management, Edersheim writes, "We have to retool our schools so that students don't simply learn how to answer multiple-choice questions. They need to synthesize information and think critically."[22] Edersheim suggested that many of the skill sets that are deemed critical for the business climate of the future are cultivated in free play and in the playful learning of childhood.[23] In play, children learn to get along and manage conflict— abilities that are critical in business environments that require work in social teams. In play, children learn not only to follow but to initiate, to bend the rules and think flexibly (making boxes into cars), and to regulate their own time. Of course, excellent preschool education by itself is insufficient to guarantee these skills.

In April and May of 2006, a collaborative group, including The Conference Board, Corporate Voices for Working Families, Partnership for 21st Century Skills, and the Society for Human Resource Management, issued a report entitled *Are they really ready to work?*.[24] Researchers asked more than 400 employers what skills they considered most important and whether high school, 2-year college, or 4-year college graduates had these desired skills. It is interesting that the top five ranked skills included oral communication, teamwork, professionalism, written communication, and critical thinking or problem solving. Creativity and innovation also made the list of skills that 81% of employers deemed very important. The report quotes J. Willard Marriott, Jr., Chairman and CEO of Marriott International, Inc. as saying, "To succeed in today's workplace, young people need more than basic reading and math skills. They need substantial content knowledge and information technology skills; advanced thinking skills, flexibility to adapt to change; and interpersonal skills to succeed in multi-cultural, cross-function teams."[25] Only 24% of the current 4-year college graduates were rated as excellent in the skills needed for today's business climate. Yet these skills are reinforced in playful learning.

The 2005 National Study of Employers released by the Family and Work Institute found similar results. Neither teaching to the test nor having preschool children sit in rows and do worksheets creates the skill set and diverse thinking styles needed to conquer 21st-century challenges. Solitary worker bees should not be our model for educational environments when the workplace is becoming a patchwork of problem solving with associates that span the globe. Indeed, recent research by Page, published in his book entitled, *The Difference: How the Power of Diversity Creates Better Groups, Firms, Schools and Societies,* indicates that distinct ways of thinking and problem solving are absolutely essential for all sorts of venues (as the title indicates).[26] Page created a mathematical model (with Lu Hong) that examined strength in organizations based on either a diverse group of employees or a group of employees with similar backgrounds. In all areas of problem solving, the diverse group outperformed the more homogeneous group. In *The New York Times* review of his book, Page commented, "The reason: diverse groups got stuck less often than the smart individuals, who tended to think similarly."[27]

Playful preschool environments do not guarantee that children will be ready for the workforce. They do, however, begin to instill a learning style that promotes lifelong learning and that prepare children with strategies that can serve them throughout their school career and beyond.

CONCLUSION

When the Association for Supervision and Curriculum Development convened the Commission on the Whole Child to recast "the definition of a successful learner from one whose achievement is measured solely by academic tests" to one that incorporates emotional and physical health and considers whether the child can function outside the classroom, they concluded that:

Although there have been some gains in student achievement, the pace of the progress is far too slow. Vast numbers of low-income and minority youngsters, in particular, continue to languish below grade level. *We believe achievement will increase when the whole child is invited and able to learn* [italics added].[28]

One way to invite the whole child to learn is through free play and playful learning. Play and playful learning offer a foundation for building strong academic and social skills but also prepare our children for the future workplace in which lifelong learners will be rewarded. Children in preschool today will be the work force of tomorrow. How will we best support them? We must return play to childhood and ensure that as we add more content into our preschool curricula, we commit to guided, but playful learning. The data suggest that if preschool pedagogy is consistent with the scientific findings, children need the opportunity to participate in free play; to be treated as whole children with brains and hearts; and to experience their learning in a playful, engaging way. Play and learning are not incompatible. Taken together, these facts offer a mandate for playful learning in preschool education and plant the seeds for lifelong learning.

Recommendations for
Policy and Practice

Play and playful learning promote all aspects of early childhood psychological development and, in so doing, provide the springboard for successful academic and social adjustment to school. Early childhood programs that squeeze out spontaneous and guided play in favor of formalized academic training dampen children's enthusiasm and motivation to learn and fail to equip children with the full range of capacities they need to thrive at school. Furthermore, lifelong learners are not created through overly didactic curricula where children are passive recipients. Returning play to its evidence-based, rightful place in early education—center-stage in the curriculum—is a first step toward restoring developmentally appropriate play experiences to children's home lives, as parents look to educators for advice and models of development-enhancing learning activities.

The following policies and practice recommendations are directed to all those who are concerned with the well-being of children and who are charged with preparing our children to become competent, contributing, and contented members of the global world:

- Policy makers and foundations
- Pediatricians and other professionals working with families
- Professional educators (and the people who train them)
- Academic researchers

Recommendation 1: Disseminate research-based, accessible information to parents and the general public on the vital role of play in learning.

- *Policy makers and foundations:*
  - Must promote public awareness and understanding of how both free play and playful learning afford academic, emotional, social, and health benefits to young children by funding the creation of pamphlets, books, newspaper op-ed pieces, TV and radio public service announcements and programs, Web sites, and other educative media. These materials, prepared by or with intensive oversight of experts in early childhood, are essential for spreading the word about the evidenced-based research on the importance of play.
- *Pediatricians and other professionals working with families:*
  - Must reinforce the message that play and learning are not mutually exclusive. A current cultural barrier to increasing children's playful experiences is the widespread but erroneous belief that "play is fun" and "learning is essential work."
  - Following the American Academy of Pediatrics, should correct the related erroneous message

that "educational toys" that prompt one right answer encourage playful learning. Combating these stereotypes, which fuel an emphasis on structured academic tutoring and scripted learning to the neglect of stimulating, playful learning in homes and preschools alike, demands immediate attention in dissemination efforts.

- Must provide parents with information on the value of play-based learning, including age-related recommendations of play activities and materials that support development, through hospital delivery room packages and pediatrician's offices. Such practices reinforce these messages.

- *Professional educators and academic researchers:*
  - Must advocate parenting and teaching practices that are research based and that conform to best developmental practices like those supported by National Association for the Education of Young Children (see http://www.naeyc.org/about/positions.asp).
  - Must train a new generation of scholars in doctoral programs who bring the evidence on free play and playful learning before the public in a way that makes the findings clear while maintaining scientific integrity.[29]

Recommendation 2: Broaden the definition of evidence-based learning.

- *Policy makers and foundations:*
  - Must change the definition of "evidence" to include the full universe of research strategies used in the developmental and learning sciences. As with studies of parenting practices[30] and media violence[31], a *combination* of correlational, experimental, and intervention research offers

the strongest case for play and playful learning. Because each methodological approach contributes uniquely,[32] the *weight of the evidence* as a whole is the most trustworthy basis for generating curricular policy and practice.

Recommendation 3: Demand, through licensing and accreditation standards, that preschool/kindergarten academic curricula follow the seven principles presented on page 59 on how young children learn best.

- *Policy makers and foundations:*
  - Must become familiar with accreditation standards and work to create and support preschool systems that are "evidence-based."
- *Professional educators:*
  - Must implement early childhood programs that accentuate activity and exploration and that minimize time spent in passive listening and repetition.
  - Must design meaningful learning experiences that integrate subject matter areas and that connect with the everyday lives of children and families.
  - Must present academic subjects such as reading and math in a stimulating, enjoyable, playful manner that engages and motivates children.
  - Must organize early childhood classroom spaces into richly prepared activity areas, including dramatic play, blocks, science, math, table games, puzzles, books, art, music, and outdoor play—each with materials and equipment in sufficient variety to meet the diverse developmental needs of individual children. It is necessary to recognize that *both* indoor and outdoor play foster academic mastery.

Recommendation 4: Maximize children's social development in preschool/kindergarten programs.

- *Professional educators and academic researchers:*
  - Must provide ample time each day in preschool/kindergarten programs for child choice of activities as well as dramatic play and free play so that children can acquire the initiative, self-control, risk taking, and social skills necessary to succeed in school, both academically and socially.
  - Must recognize that for children who are culturally diverse and perhaps speak another language, social interaction in the form of free and dramatic play allows children to use their imagination and play engagements to improve their language skills. For observant teachers, free and dramatic play can also reveal children's strengths that might not be revealed in standard assessments.

Recommendation 5: Improve educational preparation of early childhood administrators and teachers.

- *Professional educators and academic researchers:*
  - Must provide teachers with high levels of education in child development, including research-based knowledge on the importance of play and playful learning. Courses in child development and play-based learning should be mandated for associate's and bachelor's degrees in early childhood education and for early childhood teacher certification.
  - Must help teachers become astute observers of young children who are aware of children's varying developmental levels and who provide for individual differences in classroom learning

experiences by encouraging teacher training in well researched and tested programs such as Classroom Assessment Scoring System (CLASS).[33]

- Must teach teachers to appreciate the myriad emergent opportunities for learning that occur everyday in the classroom (e.g., preparing a shopping list for a trip to a make-believe store, measuring ingredients to make play dough), rather than relying on worksheets and tests to prod and demonstrate learning.

Recommendation 6: Improve preschool assessment.

- *Policy makers and foundations:*
  - Must direct funding toward the creation of preschool assessment measures with indicators of learning that have the following essential features:[34]
    - ○ Valid and reliable predictors of both *what* and *how* children learn.
    - ○ Sensitivity to the whole child. Just as integrated curricula should cross domain boundaries, assessments should be integrative such that language, reading, and mathematics are assessed in one instrument.
    - ○ Usefulness for guiding educators in selecting and implementing strong pedagogical practices.

Recommendation 7: Build connections among home, preschool, and community that foster play and playful learning.

- *Policy makers and foundations:*
  - Must create funding opportunities for parents, community organizations (e.g., libraries,

YMCAs) to collaborate around play and play-ful learning programs that support academic, health, and social outcomes for young children.

- Must work with different community stake-holders on these issues—parents, educators, principals, community centers—to build aware-ness of the evidence of the importance of play for children's learning and development. Hold-ing conferences, writing editorials for local and national newspapers, and speaking at meetings for parents and teachers are effective ways to disseminate information about play.

- *Pediatricians and educators:*
  - Should help parents of preschoolers appre-ciate the role of play in learning, both in the classroom and in the home. Send home descrip-tions of play-based classroom activities as well as suggested play-based activities to do in the home that require involvement of family mem-bers and guided play. Recognize that cultural beliefs may differ on the value of play-based learning. Work to reassure parents—based on the evidence—that play-based learning is effec-tive for academic, social-emotional, and physi-cal development.

Notes

CHAPTER ONE

1. For example, see Golinkoff & Hirsh-Pasek (1999).
2. Moore & Waltman (20070; National Education Association (2007); Neal (2007); Wisconsin Department of Public Instruction (2006).
3. Sigel (1987).
4. Hirsh-Pasek & Golinkoff (2003).
5. For example, see Bruer (1999); Silberg (2000).
6. Kaiser Foundation Report (2005).
7. Ramey & Ramey (1999); Schweinhart (2004).
8. For example, see Barnett (1998).
9. For example, see Bowman, Donovan, & Burns (2001); Bredekamp & Copple (1997).
10. For example, see Gibson & Levin (1975); Zigler & Bishop-Josef (2004).
11. For example, see Clements & Sarama (2007); Ginsburg, 2006; Jordan, Kaplan, Nabors Olah, & Locuniak (2006).
12. Ginsburg, Lee, & Boyd (2008).
13. Ramani & Siegler (in press).
14. Diamond, Barnett, Thomas, & Munro (2007).
15. Hirsh-Pasek, Kochanoff, Newcombe, & deVilliers (2005).

16. Kronholz (2005), p. B1.

17. Bodrova & Leong (2003); Brandon (2002); Murline (2000); Pellegrini (2005);Vail (2003); Zigler & Bishop-Josef (2004, 2006).

18. Meisels & Atkins-Burnett (2004); Raver & Zigler (2004); Zigler & Bishop-Josef (2006).

19. Frean (2007).

20. House (2007).

21. Bowman, Donovan, & Burns (2001); Bransford, Barron, Pea, Meltzoff, Kuhl, Bell, et al. (2006); Bransford, Brown, & Cocking (2000); Bredekamp & Copple (1997); Phillips & Shonkoff (2000); Sawyer (2006).

22. Russell & Lacoste-Caputo (2006).

23. Steinhauser (2005).

24. Gilliam (2005).

25. Belkin (2006).

26. Fisher, Hirsh-Pasek, Golinkoff, & Glick (2008).

27. Chudacoff (2007).

28. Cohen (2007).

29. Elkind (2007).

30. Ritchel & Stone (2007).

31. Elkind (2007), p. 19.

32. For example, see Berk (2001); Olfman (2005); Singer & Singer (2005).

33. Fisher, Hirsh-Pasek, Golinkoff, & Glick (2008).

34. Singer, Singer, D'Agostino, & Mallikarjun (2007).

35. Kaiser Foundation Report (2005).

36. Parish-Morris, Hirsh-Pasek, Golinkoff, & Collins (2008).

37. Storch & Whitehurst (2001); Wasik & Bond (2001).

38. Ginsberg and a distinguished committee (2006), p. 1.

39. See note 38.

40. Henig (2008).

41. Berk (2001, 2006).

42. Olfman (2005); Smith (2006).

CHAPTER TWO

1. Frost,(1969), p. 58.

2. Nourot (2004); Zigler & Bishop-Josef (2004).

3. Hirsh-Pasek & Golinkoff (2003).

4. Stecher (2002).

5. Kagan & Lowenstein (2004); Kagan, Moore, & Bredekamp (1995).

6. Hirsh-Pasek & Bruer (2007); Stern (2005).

7. Froebel (1897); Piaget (1970), among others.

8. Zigler (2007), p. 10.

9. Vygotsky (1986).

10. Roskos & Christie (2002, 2004).

11. Zigler & Bishop-Josef (2004).

12. Singer, Golinkoff, & Hirsh-Pasek (2006).

13. Datta, McHalle, & Mitchell (1976).

14. National Association for the Education of Young Children (2006), p. 8.

15. Senechal & LeFevre (2002).

16. Bowman, Donovan, & Burns (2001); Snow, Tabors, & Dickinson (2001).

17. Bodrova & Leong, 2003; Brandon, 2002; Johnson, 1998; Murline, 2000; Vail (2003); Zigler & Bishop-Josef (2004, 2006).

18. Howes & Wishard (2004),

19. Howes (1998).

20. Bodrova & Leong (2003), p. 12.

21. Zigler & Bishop-Josef (2004).

22. Raver (2002), p. 1.

23. Birch & Ladd (1997); Ladd, Birch, & Buhs (1999); Ladd, Kochenderfer, & Coleman, (1997).

24. Birch & Ladd (1997).

25. Hamre & Pianta (2001).

26. Konold & Pianta (2005).

27. Ladd, Herald, & Kochel (2006).

28. Campbell, Pungello, Miller-Johnson, Burchinal, & Ramey (2001); Campbell & Ramey (1995); Campbell, Ramey, Pungello, Sparling, & Miller-Johnson (2002).

29. Schweinhart (2004); Weikart (1998).

30. Reynolds, Ou, & Topitzes (2004).

31. Galinsky (2006).

32. Piaget (1962); Vygotsky (1986).

33. For example, see Fiese (1990).

34. Mallory & New (1994), National Association for the Education of Young Children (2006).

35. Christie & Johnsen (1983), p. 93.

36. Smith (2002), p. 5.
37. Pelligrini & Holmes (2006).
38. Belsky & Most (1981).
39. For example, see Piaget (1962).
40. McLoyd (1983).
41. McLoyd (1980).
42. Fein (1981).
43. Fein (1981); Garvey (1977).
44. Fein (1981).
45. Garvey (1977).
46. Haight & Miller (1993).
47. Zukow-Goldring (2002).
48. For example, see Smolucha & Smolucha (1998).
49. Shmuckler (1981).
50. Fiese (1990).
51. Stilson & Harding (1997).
52. Christie & Johnsen (1983); Garvey (1977); Hirsh-Pasek & Golinkoff (2003).
53. Bodrova & Leong (2007); Diamond, Barnett, Thomas, & Munro (2007).
54. Smith & Vollstedt (1985).
55. Smith (2002).
56. Tobin, Karasaw, & Hsueh (2004).
57. Lillard & Else-Quest (2006).
58. Diamond, Barnett, Thomas, & Munro (2007).
59. Blair & Razza (2007); Duncan et al. (2007); Gathercole et al. (2005).
60. Bodrova & Leong (2007).
61. See note 58, p. 1388.
62. Konold & Pianta (2005); Scarborough (2001).
63. Bergen & Mauer (2000).
64. Bruner (1983).
65. See note 64, p. 65; see also Bruner (1982); Johnson, Christie, & Wardle (2005); Wells (1983).
66. Pellegrini & Galda (1990).
67. Dickinson & Moreton (1991).
68. Dickinson & Tabors (2001).
69. See note 68, p. 253.
70. Roskos & Christie (2004), p. 116.
71. Bergen & Mauer (2000).

72. Christie & Enz (1992); Christie & Roskos (2006).

73. Zimmerman, Christakis, & Meltzoff (in press).

74. Neuman & Roskos (1992, 1993).

75. See also Kavanaugh & Engel (1998).

76. Bellin & Singer (2006).

77. Hall (2000); Justice & Pullen (2003); Katz (2001).

78. Roskos & Christie (2004), p. 116.

79. Johnson, Christie, & Wardle (2005).

80. Ness & Farenga (2007).

81. See Baroody, Lai, & Mix (2006); Geary (1994); Ginsburg, Cannon, Eisenband, & Pappas (2005); Leeb-Lundberg (1996); Nunes & Bryant (1996).

82. Seo & Ginsburg (2004).

83. Clements, Swaminathan, Hannibal, & Sarama (1999); Corsaro (1988).

84. Shallcross, Newcombe, Hirsh-Pasek, McLoyd, & Golinkoff (manuscript submitted for publication).

85. Dirks (1982); Maynard, Subrahmanyam, & Greenfield (2005).

86. Baenninger & Newcombe (1995).

87. Gelman (2006).

88. See note 87, p. 129.

89. Ramani & Siegler (in press).

90. Ginsburg, Lee, & Boyd (2008).

91. See note 90, p. 7.

92. Clemens & Samara (2007), p. 138.

93. Ruff & Capozzoli (2003); Ruff & Lawson (1990); Ruff, Lawson, Parinello, & Weissberg (1990).

94. DeLoache (2002); Golomb & Galasso (1995).

95. Newman (1990).

96. Kagan & Lowenstein (2004).

97. Bodrova & Leong (2007); Diamond, Barnett, Thomas, & Munro (2007).

98. Schultz & Bonawitz (2007).

99. Smith & Dutton (1979).

100. For example, see Diamond, Barnett, Thomas, & Munro (2007).

101. Raver (2002), p. 3.

102. Vygotsky (1978/1930–1935).

103. See note 102.

104. Connolly & Doyle (1984); Howes (1998); Howes & Matheson (1992); Hughes & Dunn (1998); Raver (2002); Singer & Singer (2005): Smith (2003).

105. Bodrova & Leong (1996); Kraft & Berk (1998); Singer & Singer (2005).

106. Barnett & Storm (1981).

107. Barnett (1984).

108. Brown, Donelan-McCall, & Dunn (1996); Hughes & Dunn (1998).

109. Youngblade & Dunn (1995).

110. Hughes & Dunn (1998).

111. Brown & Dunn (1996); Dunn, Brown, & Maguire (1995); Fabes, Eisenberg, Hanish, & Spinrad (2001).

112. Singer & Singer (2004).

113. Elias & Berk (2002).

114. Smilansky & Shefatya (1990).

115. Haight, Black, Jacobsen, & Sheridan (2006).

116. Priessler (2006).

117. Smilansky (1968).

118. See note 117, p. 25.

119. Saltz & Johnson (1974).

120. Saltz, Dixon, and Johnson (1977).

121. See note 120.

122. Dansky (1980).

123. Kagan & Lowenstein (2004), p. 74.

124. For reviews, see Hirsh-Pasek & Golinkoff (2003); Renninger & Sigel, 2006.

125. Bredekamp (2004), p. 170.

126. Berk (2006), p. 627 [italics added].

127. For example, see Bereiter (1986).

128. Bredekamp & Copple (1997).

129. Hart, Burts, & Charlesworth (1997).

130. Burts, Hart, Charlesworth, Fleege, Mosley, & Thomasson (1992); Burts, Hart, Charlesworth, & Kirk (1990); Love, Ryer, & Faddeis (1992).

131. Bryant, Burchinal, Lau, & Sparling (1994); Marcon (1993).

132. Marcon (1994).

133. Hirsh-Pasek (1991); Stipek, Feiler, Byler, Ryan, Milburn, & Salmon (1998); Stipek, Feiler, Daniels, & Milburn (1995).

134. Datta, McHalle, & Mitchell (1976).
135. For example, see Bereiter (1986); Grossen (1995).
136. Bryant, Burchinal, Lau, & Sparling (1994).
137. Caldwell & Bradley (1984).
138. Marcon (1993, 1994).
139. Assel, Landry, Swank, & Gunnewig (2007).
140. See 139, p. 472.
141. Hart, Burts, Durland, Charlesworth, DeWolf, & Fleege (1998).
142. Burts, Hart, Charlesworth, & Kirk (1990).
143. Burts, Hart, Charlesworth, Fleege, Mosley, & Thomasson (1992).
144. Schweinhart (2005); Schweinhart, Weikart & Larner (1986); but see Bereiter (1986); Mills, Cole, Jenkins, & Dale (2002).
145. Rescorla, Hyson, & Hirsh-Pasek (1991).
146. Hyson (1991); Hyson, Hirsh-Pasek, & Rescorla (1990).
147. For example, see the *Academic Skills Inventory,* Boehm & Slater (1981).
148. The Torrance Test of Preschool Creative Thinking, Torrance (1980).
149. The Pictorial Scale of Perceived Competence and Social Acceptance in Young Children, Harter & Pike (1984).
150. Hirsh-Pasek (1991).
151. Stipek, Feiler, Daniels, & Milburn (1995).
152. Ackerman, Izard, Koback, Brown, & Smith (2007).
153. Stipek, Feiler, Byler, Ryan, Milburn, & Salmon (1998).
154. See note 153.
155. Frede & Barnett (1992).
156. High Scope (2007).
157. Hart, Yang, Charlesworth, & Burt (2003).
158. Peisner-Feinberg et al. (2001).
159. See also Peisner-Feinberg, Burchinal, Clifford, Culkin, Howes, Kagan, et al. (2001).
160. Bowman, Donovan, & Burns (2001).
161. Rescorla, Hyson, & Hirsh-Pasek (1991); Stipek (1995).
162. Stipek (1995).
163. Assel, Landry, Swank, & Gunnewig, (2007); Clemens & Sarama (2007); Ginsburg (2006); Ginsburg, Lee, & Boyd (2008).
164. Zigler, Gillam, & Jones (2006).

165. Heckman & Masterov (2004).

166. Kagan & Lowenstein (2004), p. 72.

167. For example, see Hart, Yang, Charlesworth, & Burts (2003).

168. American Academy of Pediatrics (2006), p. 19.

169. Zigler (2007).

170. Sternberg (1998).

CHAPTER THREE

1. Hirsh-Pasek & Bruer (2007); Stern (2005).

2. Dehaene (2007);Stern (2005); Shaywitz (2003).

3. Hirsh-Pasek & Bruer (2007).

4. Phillips & Shonkoff (2000).

5. Bowman, Donovan, & Burns (2001).

6. Bransford, Brown, & Cocking (2000).

7. Berk (2000).

8. Zigler, Singer, & Bishop-Josef (2004).

9. Hirsh-Pasek & Golinkoff (2003).

10. Sawyer (2006).

11. Diamond, Barnett, Thomas, & Munro (2007).

12. Lillard & Else-Quest (2006).

13. For example, see Galinsky (2006).

14. Hart & Risley (1995).

15. Berk (2006).

16. Zigler (2007), p. 11.

17. Christie & Roskos (2006); Christie & Enz (1992), among others.

18. Bellin & Singer (2006).

19. Bransford, Brown, & Cocking (2000), p. 235.

20. Pink (2005), p. 1.

21. Edersheim (2007).

22. See note 21, p. 38.

23. Edersheim, personal communication, 2007.

24. Cavanaugh, Klein, Kay, & Meisinger (2006).

25. See note 24, p. 24.

26. Page (2008).

27. Dreyfus (2008).

28. Commission on the Whole Child, 2008, p. 4.

29. Zigler, Finn-Stevenson, & Hall (2002).

30. Collins, Maccoby, Steinberg, Hetherington, & Bornstein (2000).

31. Anderson, Berkowitz, Donnerstein, Huesmann, Johnson, Linz et al., (2003).

32. Miller (2007).

33. Pianta, LaParo, & Hamre (2008).

34. Hirsh-Pasek et al. (2005).

Bibliography

Ackerman, B., Izard, C., Kobak, R., Brown, E., & Smith, C. (2007).
The relation between reading problems and internalizing behavior in school for preadolescent children from economically
disadvantaged families. *Child Development, 78,* 581–596.

Anderson, C. A., Berkowitz, L., Donnerstein, E., Huesmann, R.,
Johnson, J. D., Linz, D., Malamuth, N. M., & Wartella, E.
(2003). The influence of media violence on youth. *Psychological Science in the Public Interest, 4,* 81–106.

Assel, M. A., Landry, S. H., Swank, P. R., & Gunnewig, S.
(2007). An evaluation of curriculum, setting, and mentoring
on the performance of children enrolled in pre-kindergarten.
Reading and Writing, 20, 463–494.

Baenninger, M. A., & Newcombe, N. (1995). Environmental
input to the development of sex-related differences in spatial and mathematical ability. *Learning and Individual Differences, 7,* 363–379.

Balfanz, R., Legters, N., West, T. C., & Weber, L. M. (2007). Are
NCLB's measures, incentives, and improvement strategies
the right ones for the nation's low-performing high schools?
American Educational Research Journal, 44, 559–593.

Barnett, L. A., & Storm, B. (1981). Play, pleasure, and pain: The reduction of anxiety through play. *Leisure Sciences, 2,* 161–175.

Barnett, M. A. (1984). Similarity of experience and empathy in preschoolers. *Journal of Genetic Psychology, 2,* 241–250.

Barnett, W. S. (1998). Long-term cognitive and academic effects of early childhood education on children in poverty. *Preventive Medicine, 27,* 204–207.

Baroody, A. J., Lai, M. L., & Mix, K. S. (in press). The development of young children's number and operation sense and its implications for early childhood education. In O. Saracho & B. Spodek (Eds.), *Handbook of research on the education of young children.* Mahwah, NJ: Lawrence Erlbaum Associates.

Bellin, H. & Singer, D. G. (2006). My magic story car: Video based play intervention to strengthen the emergent literacy of at risk preschoolers. In D. G. Singer, R. M. Golinkoff, & K. Hirsh-Pasek (Eds.), *Play=learning: How play motivates and enhances children's cognitive and social-emotional growth* (pp. 101–123). New York: Oxford University Press.

Belkin, D. (2006). Bringing up Einstein. *The Boston Globe.* Retrieved February 19, 2006, from http://www.boston.com/news/local/articles/2006/02/19/bringing_up_einstein/

Belsky, J., & Most, R. J. (1981). From exploration to play: A cross-sectional study of infant free play behavior. *Developmental Psychology, 17,* 630–639.

Bereiter, C. (1986). Does direct instruction cause delinquency? *Early Childhood Research Quarterly, 3,* 289–292.

Bergen, D., & Mauer, D. (2000). Symbolic play, phonological awareness, and literacy skills at three age levels. In K. A. Roskos & J. F. Christie (Eds.), *Play and literacy in early childhood: Research from multiple perspectives* (pp. 45–62). New York: Lawrence Erlbaum Associates.

Berk, L. E. (2001). *Awakening children's minds: How parents and teachers can make a difference.* New York: Oxford University Press.

Berk, L. E. (2006). *Child development* (7th ed.). Boston: Allyn & Bacon.

Berk, L. E. (2006). Make-believe play: Wellspring for development of self-regulation. In D. G. Singer, R. M. Golinkoff, &

K. Hirsh-Pasek (Eds.), *Play = learning: How play motivates and enhances children's cognitive and social-emotional growth* (pp. 74–100). New York: Oxford University Press.

Berk, L. E., Mann, T. D., & Ogan, A. T. (2006). Make-believe play: Wellspring for development of self-regulation. In D. Singer, R. M. Golinkoff, & K. Hirsh-Pasek (Eds.), *Play = learning: How play motivates and enhances children's cognitive and social-emotional growth* (pp. 74–101). New York: Oxford University Press.

Birch, S. H., & Ladd, G. W. (1997). The teacher–child relationship and children's early school adjustment. *Journal of School Psychology, 35,* 61–79.

Blair, C., & Razza, R. P. (2007). Relating effortful control, executive function, and false-belief understanding to emerging math and literacy ability in kindergarten. *Child Development, 78,* 647–663.

Bodrova, E., & Leong, D. J. (1996). *Tools of the mind: The Vygotskian approach to early childhood education.* Englewood Cliffs, NJ: Prentice Hall.

Bodrova, E. & Leong, D. J. (2003). Chopsticks and counting chips: Do play and the foundational skills need to compete for the teacher's attention in an early childhood classroom? *Young Children, 58,* 10–17.

Bodrova, E., & Leong, D. J. (2007) *Tools of the mind: The Vygotskian approach to early childhood education* (2nd edition). Upper Saddle River, NJ: Prentice Hall.

Boehm, A. E. & Slater, B. R. (1981). *Cognitive skills assessment battery.* (2nd Ed). New York: Teachers College Press.

Bowman, B., Donovan, S., & Burns, M. S. (2001). *Eager to learn.* Washington, DC: National Academy Press.

Bracey, G. W. (2006). The condition of public education. *Phi Delta Kappan, 88,* 151–165.

Brandon, K. (2002, October 20). Kindergarten less playful as pressure to achieve grows. *Chicago Tribune,* p. 1.

Bransford, J. D., Barron, B., Pea, R., Meltzoff, A., Kuhl, P., Bell, P., et al. (2006). Foundations and opportunities for an interdisciplinary science of learning. In R. K. Sawyer (Ed.), *Cambridge handbook of the learning sciences* (pp. 19–34). New York: Cambridge University Press.

Bransford, J. D., Brown, A. L., & Cocking, R. R. (Eds.). (2000). *How people learn.* Washington, DC: National Academy Press.

Bredekamp, S. (2004). Play and school readiness. In E. Zigler, D. Singer, & J. Bishop-Josef (Eds.), *Children's play: The roots of reading* (pp. 159–174). Washington, DC: Zero to Three Press.

Bredekamp, S., & Copple, C. (Eds.). (1997). *Developmentally appropriate practice in early childhood programs* (Rev. ed.). Washington, DC: National Association for the Education of Young Children.

Brennan, R. T., Kim, J., Wenz-Gross, M., & Siperstein, G. N. (2001). The relative equitability of high-stakes testing versus teacher-assigned grades: An analysis of the Massachusetts Comprehensive Assessment System (MCAS). *Harvard Educational Review, 71,* 173–216.

Brown, J. R., Donelan-McCall, N., & Dunn, J. (1996). Why talk about mental states? The significance of children's conversations with friends, siblings, and mothers. *Child Development, 67,* 836–849.

Brown, J. R., & Dunn, J. (1996). Continuities in emotion understanding from 3 to 6 years. *Child Development, 67,* 789–802.

Bruer, J. (1999). *The myth of the first three years: A new understanding of early brain development and lifelong learning.* New York: The Free Press.

Bruner, J. (1982). The formats of language acquisition. *American Journal of Semiotics, 1*(3), 1–16.

Bruner, J. (1983). *Child's talk: Learning to use language.* New York: Norton Publishers.

Bryant, D. M., Burchinal, M., Lau, L. B., & Sparling, J. J. (1994). Family and classroom correlation of Head Start children's developmental outcomes. *Early Childhood Research Quarterly, 9,* 289–309.

Burts, D. C., Hart, C. H., Charlesworth, R., Fleege, P., Mosley, J., & Thomasson, R. H. (1992). Observed activities and stress behaviors of children in developmentally appropriate and inappropriate kindergarten classrooms. *Early Childhood Research Quarterly, 7,* 297–318.

Burts, D. C., Hart, C. H., Charlesworth, R., & Kirk, L. (1990). A comparison of frequencies of stress behaviors observed in kindergarten in classrooms with developmentally appropriate versus inappropriate instructional practices. *Early Childhood Research Quarterly, 5,* 407–423.

Caldwell, B. M., & Bradley, R. H. (1984). *Home Observation for Measurement of the Environment.* Little Rock: University of Arkansas Press.

Campbell, F. A., Pungello, E. P., Miller-Johnson, S., Burchinal, M., & Ramey, C. T. (2001). The development of cognitive and academic abilities: Growth curves from an early childhood education experiment. *Developmental Psychology, 37,* 231–242.

Campbell, F. A., & Ramey, C. T. (1995). Cognitive and school outcomes for high-risk African-American students at middle adolescence: Positive effects of early intervention. *American Educational Research Journal, 32,* 743–772.

Campbell, F. A., Ramey, C. T., Pungello, E. P., Sparling, J., & Miller-Johnson, S. (2002). Early childhood education: Young adult outcomes from the Abecedarian Project. *Applied Developmental Science, 6,* 42–57.

Cavanagh, R., Klein, D., Kay, K., & Meisinger, S.R. (2006) *Ready to work: Employers perspectives on the basic knowledge and applied skills of new entrants to the 21st century U.S. workforce.* New York: The Conference Board, Corporate Voices, Partnership for 21st Century Skills, Society for Human Resource Management.

Christie, J. F., & Enz, B. (1992). The effects of literacy play interventions on preschoolers' play patterns and literacy development. *Early Education and Development, 3,* 205–220.

Christie, J., & Johnsen, E. (1983). The role of play in social-intellectual development. *Review of Educational Research, 53,* 93–115.

Christie, J., & Roskos, K. (2006). Standards, science and the role of play in early literacy education. In D. Singer, R. M. Golinkoff, & K. Hirsh-Pasek (Eds.), *Play = learning: How play motivates and enhances children's cognitive and social-emotional growth* (pp. 57–73). New York: Oxford University Press.

Chudacoff, H. P. (2007). *Children at play: An American history.* New York: New York University Press.

Clements, D. H., & Sarama, J. (2007). Early childhood mathematics learning. In F. K. Lester (Ed.), *Second handbook of research on mathematics teaching and learning* (pp. 555–661). New York: Information Age Publishing.

Clements, D. H., Swaminathan, S., Hannibal, M. A. Z., & Sarama, J. (1999). Young children's concepts of shape. *Journal for Research in Mathematics Education, 30,* 192–212.

Cohen, P. (2007). Child's play has become anything but simple. *New York Times.* Retrieved August 14, 2007, from http://www.nytimes.com/2007/08/14/books/14play.html?scp = 1&sq = Cohen%2C+P.+%2B+Child%27s+Play&st = nyt

Collins, W. A., Maccoby, E. E., Steinberg, L. D., Hetherington, E. M., & Bornstein, M. H. (2000). Contemporary research on parenting: The case for nature and nurture. *American Psychologist, 55,* 218–232.

Connolly, J. A., & Doyle, A. B. (1984). Relations of social fantasy play to social competence in preschoolers. *Developmental Psychology, 20,* 797–806.

Corsaro, W. A. (1988). Peer culture in the preschool. *Theory into Practice, 27,* 19–24.

Dansky, J. L. (1980). Cognitive consequences of sociodramatic play and exploration training for economically disadvantaged preschoolers. *Journal of Child Psychology and Psychiatry, 21,* 47–58.

Darling-Hammond, L. (2007). Evaluating 'No Child Left Behind.' *The Nation.* Retrieved May 21, 2007, from http://www.thenation.com/doc/20070521/darling-hammond/2

Datta, L. E., McHalle, C., & Mitchell, S. (1976) *The effects of the Head Start classroom experience on some aspects of child development: A summary report of national evaluations, 1966–1969.* Washington, DC: Office of Child Development.

Dehaene, S. (2007). A few steps toward a science of mental life. *Mind, Brain, and Education 1,* 28–47.

DeLoache, J. (2002). Early development of the understanding and use of symbolic artifacts. In U. Goswami (Ed.), *Blackwell handbook of child cognitive development* (pp. 206–226). Malden, MA: Blackwell.

Diamond, A., Barnett, W. S., Thomas, J., & Munro, S. (2007). Preschool program improves cognitive control. *Science, 318,* 1387–1388.

Dickinson, D., & Moreton, J. (1991, April). *Predicting specific kindergarten literacy skills from 3-year-olds' preschool expe-*

riences. Paper presented at the meeting of the Society for Research in Child Development, Seattle, WA.

Dickinson, D. K., & Tabors, P. O. (Eds.). (2001). *Beginning literacy with language: Young children learning at home and school.* Baltimore: Paul H. Brookes.

Dillon, S. (2006). Schools slow in closing gaps between races. *New York Times.* Retrieved November 20, 2006 from http://www.nytimes.com/2006/11/20/education/20gap.html?scp = 1&sq = Schools+slow+in+closing+gaps+between+races

Dirks, J. (1982). The effect of a commercial game on children's block design scores on the WUSC-R IQ test. *Intelligence, 6,* 109–124.

Dreifus, C. (2008). In professors model, diversity = productivity. *New York Times.* Retrieved January 8, 2008, from http://www.nytimes.com/2008/01/08/science/08conv.html?ref = science

Duncan, G., Claessens, A., Huston, A., Pagani, L., Engel, M., Sexton, H., et al. (2007). School readiness and later achievement. *Developmental Psychology, 43,* 1428–1446.

Dunn, J., Brown, J. R., & Maguire, M. (1995). The development of children's moral sensibility: Individual differences and emotion understanding. *Developmental Psychology, 31,* 649–659.

Edersheim, E. H. (2007). *The definitive Drucker.* New York: McGraw-Hill.

Elias, C. L. & Berk, L. E. (2002). Self-regulation in young children: Is there a role for sociodramatic play? *Early Childhood Research Quarterly 17,* 216–238.

Elkind, D. (2007). *The power of play.* Cambridge, MA: Da Capo Press.

Fabes, R. A., Eisenberg, N., Hanish, L. D., & Spinrad, T. L. (2001). Preschoolers' spontaneous emotion vocabulary: Relations to liability. *Early Education and Development 12,* 11–27.

Family & Work Institute. (2005). *National Study of Employers.* New York, NY: Family and Work Institute.

Fein, G. (1981). Pretend play in childhood: An integrative review. *Child Development, 52,* 1095–1018.

Fiese, B. (1990). Playful relationships: A contextual analysis of mother–toddler interaction and symbolic play. *Child Development, 61,* 1648–1656.

Fisher, K., Hirsh-Pasek, K., Golinkoff, R. & Glick, R. (in press). Conceptual split? Parents and experts' perception of play in the 21st century. *Journal of Applied Developmental Psychology.*

Frean, A. (2007). Stealth curriculum is "threat to all toddlers." *The Times* (London). Retrieved November 30, 2007, from http://www.timesonline.co.uk/tol/life_and_style/education/article2971600.ece

Frede, E., & Barnett, W. S. (1992). Developmentally appropriate public school preschool: A study implementation of the High/Scope curriculum and its effects on disadvantaged children's skills in first grade. *Early Childhood Research Quarterly, 7,* 483–499.

Froebel, F. (1897). *Pedagogics of the kindergarten.* London: Appleton. (J. Jarvis, Trans.).

Frost, Robert. (1915). *North of Boston.* New York: Henry Holt & Co.

Galinsky, E. (2006). *The economic benefits of high quality early childhood programs: What makes the difference?* Report for the Committee on Economic Development. New York: Families and Work Institute.

Garvey, C. (1977). *Play.* Cambridge, MA: Harvard University Press.

Gathercole, S.E.,Tiffany, C., Briscoe, A., Thorn, A., ALSPAC Team. (2005). Developmental consequences of poor phonological short-term memory function in childhood: A longitudinal study. *Journal of Child Psychology and Psychiatry, 46,* 598–611.

Geary, D. C. (1994). *Children's mathematical development: Research and practical applications.* Washington, DC: American Psychological Association.

Gelman, R. (2006). Young natural–number arithmeticians. *Current Directions in Psychological Science, 15,* 193–197.

Gibson, E. J., & Levin, H. (1975). *The psychology of reading.* Cambridge, MA: MIT Press.

Gilliam, W. S. (2005). *Prekindergarteners left behind: Expulsion rates in prekindergarten programs.* FDC Policy Brief Series No. 3. New York: Foundation for Child Development.

Ginsberg, K., and committee. (2007). *The importance of play in promoting healthy child development and maintaining strong parent-child bonds. Pediatrics 119*(1) 192–191.

Ginsburg, H. (2006). Mathematical play and playful mathematics: A guide for early education. In D. Singer, R. M. Golinkoff, & K. Hirsh-Pasek (Eds.), *Play = learning: How play motivates and enhances children's cognitive and social-emotional growth* (pp. 145–165). New York: Oxford University Press.

Ginsburg, H. P., Cannon, J., Eisenband, J. G., & Pappas, S. (2005). Mathematical thinking and learning. In K. McCartney & D. Phillips (Eds.), *Blackwell handbook of early childhood development* (pp. 208–229). Oxford, UK: Blackwell.

Ginsburg, H. P., Lee, J. S., & Boyd, J. S. (2008). Mathematics education for young children: What it is and how to promote it. *SRCD Social Policy Report, XXII,* 1–23.

Golinkoff, R., & Hirsh-Pasek, K. (1999). *How babies talk: The magic and mystery of language acquisition.* New York: Dutton/Penguin.

Golomb, C., & Galasso, L. (1995). Make believe and reality: Explorations of the imaginary realm. *Developmental Psychology, 31,* 800–810.

Gormly, W., Gayer, T., Phillips, D., & Dawson, B. (2006). The effects of universal pre-k on cognitive development. *Developmental Psychology, 41,* 872–885.

Green, L. (2008). Weird science: Lessons on hold to prep for FCAT. *Palm Beach Post.* Retrieved January 30, 2008, from http://www.backyardpost.com/news/2008/jan/30/weird-science-lessons-on-hold-to-prep-for-fcat/

Grossen, B. (1995). The story behind Project Follow Through. *Effective school practices, 15.* Retrieved January 15, 2008, from http://darkwing.uoregon.edu/~adiep/ft/151toc.htm

Haight, W., Black, J., Jacobsen, T., & Sheridan, K. (2006). Pretend play and emotion learning in traumatized mothers and children. In D. Singer, R. M. Golinkoff, & K. Hirsh-Pasek (Eds.), *Play = learning: How play motivates and enhances children's cognitive and social-emotional growth* (pp. 209–230). New York: Oxford University Press.

Haight, W. L., & Miller, P. J. (1993). *Pretending at home: Early development in a sociocultural context.* Albany: State University of New York Press.

Hall, N. (2000). Literacy, play, and authentic experience. In K. A. Roskos & J. F. Christie (Eds.), *Play and literacy in early childhood: Research from multiple perspectives* (pp. 189–204). Mahwah, NJ: Lawrence Erlbaum Associates.

Hamre, B. K., & Pianta, R. C. (2001). Early teacher-child relationships and the trajectory of children's school outcomes through eighth grade. *Child Development, 72,* 625–638.

Hart, B. & Risley, T. (1995). Meaningful differences in the everyday experience of young American children. Baltimore: Brookes Publishing Co.

Hart, C. H., Burts, D. C., & Charlesworth, R. (1997). Integrated developmentally appropriate curriculum: From theory and research to practice. In C. H. Hart, D. C. Burts, & R. Charlesworth (Eds.), *Integrated curriculum and developmentally appropriate practice: Birth to age 8* (pp. 1–27). Albany, NY: State University of New York Press.

Hart, C. H., Burts, D. C., Durland, M. A., Charlesworth, R., DeWolf, M., & Fleege, P. O. (1998). Stress behaviors and activity type participation of preschoolers in more and less developmentally appropriate classrooms: SES and sex differences. *Journal of Research in Childhood Education, 12,* 176–196.

Hart, C. H., Yang, C., Charlesworth, R., & Burts, D. C. (2003). Kindergarten teaching practices: Associations with later child academic and social/emotional adjustment to school. Paper presented at the meeting of the Society for Research in Child Development, Tampa, FL.

Harter, S., & Pike, R. (1984). The pictorial scale of perceived competence and social acceptance for young children. *Child Development, 55,* 1969–1982.

Heckman, J., & Masterov, D. (2004). The productivity argument for investing in young children. *Working paper 5, Committee for economic development.*

Henig, R. M. (2008, February 17). Taking play seriously. *New York Times Magazine.*

High Scope. (2007). High/Scope Curriculum web page. Retrieved February 1, 2008, from http://www.highscope.org/Content.asp?ContentId = 223

Hirsh-Pasek, K. (1991). Pressure or challenge in preschool? How academic environments affect children. In L. Rescorla, M. C. Hyson, & K. Hirsh-Pasek (Eds.), *New directions in child development. Academic instruction in early childhood:*

Challenge or pressure? (no. 53, pp. 39–46). San Francisco: Jossey-Bass.

Hirsh-Pasek, K., & Bruer, J. (2007). The brain/education barrier. *Science, 317,* 1293.

Hirsh-Pasek, K., & Golinkoff, R. M. (2003). *Einstein never used flashcards: How our children really learn and why they need to play more and memorize less.* Emmaus, PA: Rodale Press.

Hirsh-Pasek, K., Kochanoff, A., Newcombe, N., & deVilliers, J. (2005). Using scientific knowledge to inform preschoolers: Making the case for "empirical validity." *Social Policy Report. Society for Research in Child Development, 9*(1).

Holloway, S. D. (2000). *Contested childhood: Diversity and change in Japanese preschools.* New York: Routledge.

House, R. (2007). Schooling, the state, and children's psychological well-being: A psychosocial critique. *Journal of Psychological Research, 2,* 49–62.

House, E. R., Glass, G. V., McLean, L. F., & Walker, D. F. (1978). No simple answer: Critique of the "Follow Through" evaluation. *Harvard Educational Review, 28,* 128–160.

Howes, C. (Ed.). (1998). *The earliest friendships.* New York: Cambridge University Press.

Howes, C., & Matheson, C. C. (1992). Sequences in the development of competent play with peers: Social and social pretend play. *Developmental Psychology, 28,* 961–974.

Howes, C., & Wishard, A. G. (2004). Revisiting shared meaning: Looking through the lens of culture and linking shared pretend play through proto-narrative development to emergent literacy. In E. F. Zigler, D. G. Singer, & S. Bishop-Josef (Eds.), *Children's play: The roots of reading* (pp. 143–158). Washington, DC: Zero to Three Press.

Hughes, C., & Dunn, J. (1998). Understanding mind and emotion: Longitudinal associations with mental-state talk between young friends. *Developmental Psychology, 34,* 1026–1037.

Hursh, D. (2007). Assessing No Child Left Behind and the rise of neoliberal education policies. *American Educational Research Journal, 44,* 493–518.

Hyson, M. (1991). The characteristics and origins of the academic preschool. In L. Rescorla, M. C. Hyson, & K. Hirsh-Pasek (Eds.), *New directions in child development. Academic instruction in early childhood: Challenge or pressure?* (no. 53, pp. 39–46). San Francisco: Jossey-Bass.

Hyson, M., Hirsh-Pasek, K., & Rescorla, L. (1990) The classroom practice inventory: An observation instrument based on NAEYC's Guidelines for Developmentally Appropriate Practices for 4- and 5-year old children. *Early Childhood Research Quarterly, 5*(4), 475–495.

Johnson, D. (1998). Many schools putting an end to child's play. *New York Times.* Retrieved from April 7, 1998, from http:// query.nytimes.com/gst/fullpage.html?res = 9506E0DB1E3A F934A35757C0A96E958260&scp = 1&sq = Many+schools+p utting+an+end+to+child%92s+play

Johnson, J. E, Christie, J. F.& Wardle, F. (2005). *Play, development and early education.* Boston: Pearson Education.

Jordan, N. C., Kaplan, D., Nabors Olah, L., & Locuniak, M. N. (2006). Number sense growth in kindergarten: A longitudinal investigation of children at risk for mathematics difficulties. *Child Development, 77,* 153–175.

Justice, L. M., & Pullen, P. C. (2003). Promising interventions for promoting emergent literacy skills: Three evidence-based approaches. *Topics in Early Childhood Special Education, 23,* 99–113.

Kagan, S. L., & Lowenstein, A. E. (2004). School readiness and children's play: Contemporary oxymoron or compatible option? In E. F. Zigler, D. G. Singer, & S. J. Bishop-Josef (Eds), *Children's play: The roots of reading* (pp. 59–76). Washington, DC: Zero to Three Press.

Kagan, S. L., Moore, E., & Bredekamp, S. (Eds.). (1995). Reconsidering children's early development and learning: Toward common views and vocabulary (GP01995–396–664). *National Education Goals Panel,* Goal 1 Technical Planning Group. Washington, DC: Government Printing Office.

Kaiser Foundation Report (2005). *A teacher in the living room: Educational media for babies, toddlers and preschoolers.* Washington, DC: Kaiser Foundation.

Katz, J. R. (2001). Playing at home: The talk of pretend play. In D. K. Dickinson & P. O. Tabors (Eds.), *Beginning literacy with language: Young children learning at home and school* (pp. 53–73). Baltimore: Paul H. Brookes.

Kavanaugh, R. D., & Engel, S. (1998). The development of pretense and narrative in early childhood. In O. N. Saracho & B. Spodek (Eds.), *Multiple perspectives on play in early childhood education* (pp. 80–99). Albany: State University of New York Press.

Konold, T., & Pianta, R. (2005). Empirically derived, person-oriented patterns of school readiness in typically developing children: Description and prediction to first grade achievement. *Applied Developmental Science, 4,* 174–197.

Kraft, K. C., & Berk, L. E. (1998). Private speech in two preschools: Significance of open-ended activities and make-believe play for verbal self-regulation. *Early Childhood Research Quarterly, 13,* 637–658.

Kronholtz, J. (2005, July 12). Preschooler' prep—courses help kids get ready for kindergarten, which is like first grade used to be. *Wall Street Journal,* pp. B1, B4.

Ladd, G. W., Birch, S. H., & Buhs, E. S. (1999). Children's social and scholastic lives in kindergarten: Related spheres of influence? *Child Development, 70,* 1373–1400.

Ladd, G. W., Herald, S. L., and Kochel K. P. (2006). School readiness: Are there social prerequisites? *Early Education and Development, 17,* 115–150.

Ladd, G. W., Kochenderfer, B. J., & Coleman, C. C. (1997). Classroom peer acceptance, friendship, and victimization: Distinct relational systems that contribute uniquely to children's school adjustment. *Child Development, 68,* 1181–1197.

Leeb-Lundberg, K. (1996). The block builder mathematician. In E. S. Hirsh (Ed.), *The block book* (pp. 34–60). Washington, DC: National Association for the Education of Young Children.

Lillard, A., & Else-Quest, N. (2006). Evaluating Montessori education. *Science, 313,* 1893–1894.

Love, J. M., Ryer, P., & Faddeis, B. (1992). *Caring environments: Program quality in California's publicly funded child development programs.* Portsmouth, NH: RMC Research Corporation.

Mallory, B. L., & R. S. New. (1994) Social constructivist theory and principles of inclusion: Challenges for early childhood special education. *Journal of Special Education, 28,* 322–37.

Marcon, R. A. (1993). Socioemotional versus academic emphasis: Impact on kindergartners' development and achievement. *Early Child Development and Care, 96,* 81–91.

Marcon, R. A. (1994). Doing the right thing for children: Linking research and policy reform in the District of Columbia public schools. *Young Children, 50,* 8–20.

Maynard, A. E., Subrahmanyam, K., & Greenfield, P. M. (2005). Technology and the development of intelligence. In R. J. Sternberg & D. Preiss (Eds.), *Intelligence and technology: The impact of tools on the nature and development of human abilities* (pp. 54–97). Mahwah, NJ: Erlbaum.

McLoyd, V. (1980). Modes of transformation in the pretend play of black, low-income children. *Child Development, 51,* 1133–1139.

McLoyd, V. (1983). The effects of the structure of play objects on the pretend play of low-income preschool children. *Child Development, 54,* 626–635.

Meisels, S. J., & Atkins-Burnett, S. (2004). Public policy viewpoint. The Head Start national reporting system: A critique. *Young Children, 59,* 64–66.

Miller, S. A. (2007). *Developmental research methods* (3rd ed.). Newbury Park, CA: Sage.

Mills, P., Cole, K., Jenkins, J., & Dale, P. (2002). Early exposure to direct instruction and subsequent juvenile delinquency: A prospective examination. *Exceptional Children, 69,* 85–96.

Moore, J. L., & Waltman, K. (2007, April). *Pressure to increase test scores in reaction to NCLB: An investigation of related factors.* Paper presented at the meeting of the American Educational Research and Evaluation Association, Chicago, IL.

Mondoza, C. (2006). Inside today's classrooms: Teacher voices on No Child Left Behind and the education of gifted children. *Roeper Review, 29,* 28–31.

Murline, A. (May, 2000). What's your favorite class? Most kids would say recess. Yet many schools are cutting back on unstructured schoolyard play. *U.S. News and World Report, 128*(17), 50–52.

National Association for the Education of Young Children. (2006). *Principles of child development that inform developmentally appropriate practice.* Retrieved July 11, 2008, from http://www.naeyc.org/about/positions/dap3.asp

National Education Association. (2007). *NCLB/ESEA: It's time for a change! Voices from America's classrooms.* Retrieved January 8, 2007, from http://www.nea.org/esea/nclbstories/index.html

Neal, D. (2007). Left behind by design: Proficiency counts and test-based accountability. Retrieved January 15, 2008, from http://home.uchicago.edu/~n9na/web_ver_final.pdf. Unpublished manuscript, University of Chicago, Chicago.

Ness, D., & Farenga, S. J. (2007). *Knowledge under construction: The importance of play in developing children's spatial and geometric thinking.* Lanham, MD: Rowman & Littlefield Publishers.

Network, N. E. C. C. R. (2005). Pathways to reading: The role of oral language in the transition to reading. *Developmental Psychology, 41,* 428–442.

Neuman, S., & Roskos, K. (1992). Literacy objects as cultural tools: Effects on children's literacy behaviors during play. *Reading Research Quarterly, 27,* 203–223.

Newman, L. S. (1990). Intentional and unintentional memory in young children: Remembering vs. playing. *Journal of Experimental Child Psychology, 50,* 243–258.

Nichols, S. L., & Berliner, D.C. (2007). The pressure to cheat in a high-stakes testing environment. In E. M. Anderman & T. B. Murdock (Eds.), *Psychology of academic cheating* (pp. 289–311). San Francisco: Jossey-Bass.

Noble, A. (2004). Testing is not an exact science. University of Delaware, *Education Research and Development Center, Education Policy Brief, 16,* 1–9.

Nourot, P. M. (2004). Historical perspectives on early childhood education. In J. L. Roopnarine & J. E. Johnson (Eds.), *Approaches to early childhood education* (pp. 3–31). Englewood Cliffs, NJ: Prentice Hall.

Nunes, T., & Bryant, P. (1996). *Children doing mathematics.* Oxford, UK: Blackwell.

Olfman, S. (2005). Where do the children play? In S. Olfman (Ed.), *Childhood lost: How American culture is failing our kids* (pp. 203–216). Westport, CT: Praeger.

Page, S. (2007). *The difference: How the power of diversity creates better groups, firms, schools and societies.* Princeton, NJ: Princeton University Press.

Parish-Morris, J., Hirsh-Pasek, K., Golinkoff, R. M., & Collins, M. (2008). *Smarter books = smarter children?: Electronic console books and emergent literacy.* Manuscript submitted for publication.

Peisner-Feinberg, E. S., Burchinal, M. R., Clifford, R. M., Culkin, M. L., Howes, C., Kagan, S. L., et al. (2001). The relation of preschool childcare quality to children's cognitive and social development trajectories through second grade. *Child Development, 72,* 1534–1553.

Pellegrini, A. D. (2005). *Recess: Its role in development in education.* Mahwah, NJ: Lawrence Erlbaum Associates.

Pellegrini, A. D., & Galda, L. (1990). Children's play, language, and early literacy. *Topics in Language Disorders, 10,* 76–88.

Pellegrini, A. D. & Holmes, R. M. (2006). The role of recess in primary school. In D. G. Singer, R. M. Golinkoff, & K. Hirsh-Pasek (Eds.), *Play = learning: How play motivates and enhances children's cognitive and social-emotional growth* (pp. 36–53). New York: Oxford University Press.

Phillips, D., & Shonkoff, J. (2000). *From neurons to neighborhoods.* Washington, DC: National Academy Press.

Piaget, J. (1962). *Play, dreams, and imitation in childhood.* New York: Norton Publishers.

Piaget, J. (1970). *Science of education and the psychology of the child.* New York: Orion Press.

Pianta, R. C., La Paro. K. M., & Hamre, B. (2008). *Classroom Assessment Scoring System (CLASS).* Baltimore, MD: Paul H. Brookes.

Pica, P., Lemer, C., Izard, V., & Dehane, S. (2004). Exact and approximate arithmetic in an Amazonian indigenous group. *Science, 306,* 499–503.

Pink, D. H. (2005). *A whole new mind: The rise of right-brain thinking and the new way to succeed.* New York: Riverhead Books.

Porter, A. C. & Polikoff, M. S. (2007). NCLB: State interpretations, early effects, and suggestions for reauthorization. *SRCD Social Policy Report, XXI,* 3–15.

Priessler, M. (2006). Play and autism: Facilitating symbolic understanding. In D. Singer, R. M. Golinkoff, & K. Hirsh-Pasek (Eds.), *Play = learning: How play motivates and enhances children's cognitive and social-emotional growth* (pp. 231–250). New York: Oxford University Press.

Ramani, G., & Siegler, R. (in press). Promoting broad and stable improvements in low-income children's numerical knowledge through playing board games. *Developmental Science.*

Ramey, S. L., & Ramey, C. T. (1999). Early experience and early intervention for children "at risk" for developmental delay and mental retardation. *Mental Retardation and Developmental Disabilities, 5,* 1–10.

Raver, C. C. (2002). Emotions matter: Making the case for the role of young children's emotional development for early school readiness. *SRCD Social Policy Report, XVI,* 3–18.

Raver, C. C., & Zigler, E. F. (2004). Public policy viewpoint. Another step back? Assessing readiness in Head Start. *Young Children, 59,* 59–63.

Renninger, K. A., & Sigel, I. E. (2006). Child psychology research in practice. In K. A. Renninger and I. E. Sigel (Eds.), *Child Psychology in Practice* (pp. xxvii–xxix). In W. Damon and R. Lerner (Gen. Eds.), *Handbook of Child Psychology,* 6th ed. New York: John Wiley & Sons.

Rescorla, L., Hyson, M., & Hirsh-Pasek, K. (Eds.). (1991). Academic instruction in early childhood: Challenge or pressure? In W. Damon (Ed.), *New directions in developmental psychology.* New York: Jossey-Bass.

Reynolds, A., Ou, S., & Topitzes, J. W. (2004). Paths of effects if early childhood intervention on educational attainment and delinquency: A confirmatory analysis of the Chicago Child-Parent Centers. *Child Development, 75,* 1299–1328.

Ritchel, M., & Stone, B. (2007). For toddlers, toy of choice is tech device. *New York Times.* Retrieved November 29, 2007, from http://www.nytimes.com/2007/11/29/technology/29techtoys.html

Roskos, K., & Christie, J. F. (Eds.). (2002). *Play and literacy in early childhood: Research from multiple perspectives.* Mahwah, NJ: Lawrence Erlbaum Associates.

Roskos, K., & Christie, J. (2004). Examining the play-literacy interface: A critical review and future directions. In E. F. Zigler, D. G. Singer, & S. J. Bishop-Josef (Eds.), *Children's play: Roots of reading* (pp.95–123). Washington, DC; Zero to Three Press.

Ruff, H. A., & Capozzoli, M. C. (2003). Development of attention and distractibility in the first 4 years of life. *Developmental Psychology, 39,* 877–890.

Ruff, H. A., & Lawson, K. R. (1990). Development of sustained, focused attention in young children during free play. *Developmental Psychology, 26,* 85–93.

Ruff, H. A., Lawson, K. R., Parinello, R., & Weissberg, R. (1990). Long-term stability of individual differences in sustained attention in the early years. *Child Development, 61,* 60–75.

Russell, J., & LaCoste-Caputo, J. (2006). More kids repeating kindergarten. *Express-News.* Retrieved December 4, 2006, from http://www.districtadministration.com/newssummary. aspx?news = yes&postid = 17845

Ryder, R. J., Burton, J. L., & Silberg. A. (2006). Longitudinal study of direct instructon effects from first through third grade. *Journal of Educational Research, 99,* 179–191.

Sacks, P. (2005). "No child left": What are schools for in a democratic society? In S. Olfman (Ed.), *Childhood lost: How American culture is failing our kids* (pp. 185–202). Westport, CT: Praeger.

Saltz, E., Dixon, D., & Johnson, J. (1977). Training disadvantaged preschoolers on various fantasy activities: Effects on cognitive functioning and impulse control. *Child Development, 48,* 367–380.

Saltz, E., & Johnson, J. (1974). Training for thematic-fantasy play in culturally disadvantaged children: Preliminary results. *Journal of Educational Psychology, 66,* 623–630.

Sawyer, R. K. (Ed.). (2006). *Cambridge handbook of the learning sciences.* New York: Cambridge University Press.

Scarborough, H. S. (2001). Connecting early language and literacy to later reading (dis)abilities: Evidence, theory, and practice. In S. B. Neuman & D. K. Dickinson (Eds.), *Handbook of early literacy research* (pp. 97–110). New York: Guilford Press.

Schultz, L. & Bonawitz, E. B. Serious fun: Preschoolers engage in more exploratory play when evidence in confounded. *Developmental Psychology, 43,* 1045–1050.

Schweinhart, L., (2005). The High/Scope Perry Preschool study through age 40: Summary, conclusions and frequently asked questions. Ypsilanti, MI: High Scope Educational Research Foundation.

Schweinhart, L. J., Weikart, D., & Larner, M. B. (1986). Consequences of three preschool curriculum models through age 15. *Early Childhood Research Quarterly, 1,* 15–45.

Senechal, M., & LeFevre, J.-A. (2002). Parental involvement in the development of children's reading skill: A five-year longitudinal study. *Child Development, 73,* 445–461.

Seo, K.-H., & Ginsburg, H. P. (2004). What is developmentally appropriate in early childhood mathematics education? Lessons from new research. In D. H. Clements, J. Sarama, & A. M. DiBiase (Eds.), *Engaging young children in mathematics: Standards for early childhood mathematics education* (pp. 91–104). Mahwah, NJ: Lawrence Erlbaum Associates.

Shallcross, W., Newcombe, N., Hirsh-Pasek, K., McLoyd, M., & Golinkoff, R. M. Not just child's play: Block play stimulates spatial language from parents. Manuscript submitted for publication.

Shaywitz, S. (2003). *Overcoming dyslexia: A new and complete science based program for reading problems at any level.* New York: Knopf.

Shmuckler, D. (1981). Mother–child interaction and its relationship to the predisposition of imaginative play. *Genetic Psychology Monographs, 104,* 215–235.

Sigel, I. E. (1987). Does hothousing rob children of their childhood? *Early Childhood Research Quarterly, 2,* 211–225.

Silberg, J. (2000). *125 brain games for toddlers and twos: Simple games to promote early brain development.* Beltsville, MD: Gryphon House.

Singer, D. G., Golinkoff, R. M., & Hirsh-Pasek, K. (Eds.). (2006). *Play = learning: How play motivates and enhances children's cognitive and social-emotional growth.* New York: Oxford University Press.

Singer, D. G., & Singer, J. L. (2004). Encouraging school readiness through guided pretend games. In E. F. Zigler, D. G. Singer, & S. J. Bishop-Josef (Eds.), *Children's play: The roots of reading* (pp. 175–187). Washington, DC: Zero to Three Press.

Singer, D. G., & Singer, J. L.(2005). *Imagination and play in the electronic* age. Cambridge, MA; Harvard University Press.

Singer, J. L., Singer, D. G., D'Agostino, H., & Mallikarjun, R. (2007). *Giving our children the right to be children: A mother's perspective: A global report.* New York: Strategy One.

Slavin, R. E. (2002). Evidence-based education policies: Transforming educational practice and research. *Educational Researcher, 31,* 15–21.

Smilansky, S. (1968). *The effects of sociodramatic play on disadvantaged preschool children.* New York: Wiley.

Smilansky, S., & Shefatya, L. (1990). *Facilitating play: A medium for promoting cognitive, socioemotional and academic development in young children,* Gathersburg, MD: Psychosocial and Educational Publications.

Smith, P. K. (Ed.). (1984). *Play in animals and humans.* Oxford, UK: Basil Blackwell.

Smith, P. K. (2002). Pretend play, metarepresentation and theory of mind. In R. W. Mitchell (Ed.), *Pretending and imagination in animals and children* (pp. 129–141). Cambridge, MA: Cambridge University Press.

Smith, P. K. (2003). Play and peer relations. In A. Slater & G. Bremner (Eds.), *An introduction to developmental psychology* (pp. 311–333). Malden, MA: Blackwell.

Smith, P. K. (2006). Evolutionary foundations and functions of play: An overview. In A. Göncü & S. Gaskins (Eds.), *Play and development: Evolutionary, sociocultural, and functional perspectives* (pp. 21–49). Mahwah, NJ: Lawrence Erlbaum Associates.

Smith, P. K., & Dutton, S. (1979). Play and training in direct and innovative problem solving. *Child Development, 50,* 830–836.

Smith, P. K., & Vollsedt, R. (1985). On defining play: An empirical study of the relationship between play and various play criteria. *Child Development, 56,* 1042–1050.

Smolucha, L., & Smolucha, F. (1998). The social origins of mind: Post-Piagetian perspectives on pretend play. In O. N. Saracho & B. Spodek (Eds.), *Multiple perspectives on play in early childhood education* (pp. 34–58). Albany: State University of New York Press.

Snow, C. E., Tabors, P. O., & Dickinson, D. K. (2001). Language development in the preschool years. In D. K. Dickinson & P. O. Tabors (Eds.), *Beginning literacy with language: Young children learning at home and school* (pp. 1–30). Baltimore, MD: Paul H. Brooks.

Steinhauser, J. (2005, May 22). Maybe preschool is the problem. *New York Times,* Section 4, pp. 1, 4.

Stern, E. (2005). Psychology meets neuroscience. *Science, 310,* 745.

Sternberg, R. (1998, January). Teaching and assessing for successful intelligence. *The School Administrator.* Retrieved from   http://www.aasa.org/publications/saarticledetail.cfm? ItemNumber=4271

Sternberg, R. J, & Grigorenko, E. L. (2007). *Teaching for successful intelligence: To increase student learning and achievement.* New York: Plume.

Stilson, S. R., & Harding, C. G. (1997). Early social context as it relates to symbolic play: A longitudinal investigation. *Merrill-Palmer Quarterly, 43,* 682–693.

Stipek, D. (1995). The development of pride and shame in toddlers. In J. Tangney & K. Fischer (Eds.), *Self-conscious emotions: The psychology of shame, guilt, embarrassment, and pride* (pp. 237–252). New York: Guilford Press.

Stipek, D., Feiler, R., Byler, P., Ryan, R., Milburn, S., & Salmon, J. M. (1998). Good beginnings: What difference does the program make in preparing young children for school? *Journal of Applied Developmental Psychology, 19,* 41–66.

Stipek, D., Feiler, R., Daniels, D., & Milburn, S. (1995). Effects of different instructional approaches on young children's achievement and motivation. *Child Development, 66,* 209–233.

Stecher, B. M. (2002). Consequences of large-scale, high-stakes testing on school and classroom practice. In L. S. Hamilton, S. P. Klein, & B. M. Stecher Rand (Eds.), *Making sense of test-based accountability in education* (p. 79). Santa Monica, CA: Rand Corporation.

Storch, S. A., & Whitehurst, G. J. (2001). The role of family and home in the literacy development of children from low-income backgrounds. In P. R. Britto & J. Brooks-Gunn (Eds.), *The role of family literacy environments in promoting young children's emerging literacy skills* (pp. 53–71). San Francisco: Jossey-Bass.

Temple, J. A., & Reynolds, A. J. (2006). Economic returns of investments in preschool education. In E. Zigler & S. Jones (Eds.), *A vision for universal prekindergarten* (pp. 37–68). New York: Cambridge University Press.

Tobin, J., Karasaw, M., & Hsueh, Y. (2004). Komatsudani then and now: Continuity and change in a Japanese preschool. *Contemporary Issues in Early Childhood, 5,* 128–144.

Torrance, E. P. (1980). *The Torrance Tests of Creative Thinking.* New York: Scholastic Testing Service.

Treffinger, D. (2006). So many children left behind? *Creative Learning Today, 14,* 1–3.

Vail, K. (2003). Ready to learn. What the Head Start debate about early academics means for your schools. *American School Board Journal, 190.* Retrieved May 25, 2005, from http//www.asbj.com/2003/11/1103coverstory.html

Viadero, D. (2007). Teachers say NCLB has changed classroom practice. *Education Week, 26,* 6, 22.

Vygotsky, L. S. (1978). *Mind in society: The development of higher mental processes.* (M. Cole, V. John-Steiner, S. Scribner, & E. Souberman, Eds. and Trans.). Cambridge, MA: Harvard University Press. (Original work published 1930–1935).

Vygotsky, L. (1986). *Thought and language.* (A. Kozulin, Trans.). Cambridge, MA: Massachusetts Institute of Technology Press. (Original work published 1930, 1933, and 1935)

Wasik, B. A., & Bond, M. A. (2001). Beyond the pages of a book: Interactive book reading and language development in preschool classrooms. *Journal of Educational Psychology, 93,* 243–250.

Weikart, D. P. (1998). Changing early childhood development through educational intervention. *Preventive Medicine, 27,* 233–237.

Wells, G. (1983). Talking with children: The complimentary roles of parents and teachers. In M. Donaldson, R. Grieve, & C. Pratt (Eds.), *Early childhood development and education* (pp. 127–150). New York: Guilford Press.

Willenz, P. (2007, November 12). *Children's early academic and attention skills best predict later school success, according to analysis of large-scale studies.* American Psychological Association Press Release.

Winerip, M. (2006). Bitter lesson: A good school gets an 'F.' *New York Times*. Retrieved January 11, 2006, from http://www.nytimes.com/2006/01/11/education/11education.html

Wisconsin Department of Public Instruction. (2006, June 22). *Conversation Café: NCLB. Voices from Wisconsin* [Radio show].

Youngblade, L. M., & Dunn, J. (1995). Individual differences in young children's pretend play with mother and sibling: Links to relationships and understanding of other people's feelings and beliefs. *Child Development, 66,* 1472–1492.

Zigler, E. F. (2007). Giving intervention a head start: A conversation with Edward Zigler. *Educational Leadership, 65,* 8–14.

Zigler, E. F., & Bishop-Josef, S. J. (2004). Play under siege: A historical overview. In E. F. Zigler, D. G. Singer, & S. J. Bishop-Josef (Eds.), *Children's play: The roots of reading* (pp. 1–13). Washington, DC: Zero to Three Press.

Zigler, E. F. & Bishop-Josef, S. J. (2006). The cognitive child versus the whole child: Lessons from 40 years of Head Start. In D. Singer, R. Golinkoff, & K. Hirsh-Pasek (Eds.), *Play = learning: How play motivates and enhances children's cognitive and social-emotional growth* (pp. 15–35). New York: Oxford University Press.

Zigler, E. F., Finn-Stevenson, M., & Hall, N. W. (2002). *The first three years and beyond: Brain development and social policy*. New Haven: Yale University Press.

Zigler, E. F., Gillam, W., & Jones, S. (2006). *A vision for universal preschool*. Cambridge, MA: Cambridge University Press.

Zimmerman, F. J., Christakis, D. A., & Meltzoff, A. N. (in press). Associations between media viewing and language development in children under age 2 years. *Journal of Pediatrics*.

Zukow-Goldring, P. (2002). Sibling caregiving. In M. H. Bornstein (Ed.), *Handbook of parenting* (2nd ed., Vol. 3, pp. 253–286). Mahwah, NJ: Lawrence Erlbaum Associates.

Author Index

Subject Index

academic achievement/learning
    attentional focus, 36
    boot camps, 10
    as dependent variable, 44
    developmental pedagogy, 51
    direct-instruction pedagogy,
      44–46
    language/literacy, 29–33
    numeracy/spatial concepts, 33–36
    vs. social competence, 21–22
    whole-child approach, 20–21
accountability, educators, 8–9
accreditation standards,
    evidence-based learning, 70
achievement gap, underprivileged
    children, 6–8
achievement tests, 49, 64
Alliance for Childhood, *Call to
    Action on the Education
    of Young Children,* 22–23
American Academy of Pediatrics, 14,
    55, 68–69
anxiety, free play, 39
Are they really ready to work?
    (report), 63

assessments/tests
    achievement, 49, 64
    educators, 8
    mathematical improvement, 72
    standardized, 10–11, 41–42, 50
    success of, 35
    teaching to, 64
Association for Supervision and
    Curriculum Development
    (ASCD), 64–65
attentional focus
    flexibility, tasks, 11, 28–29
    lower-income children, 36
    play, role of, 36–37
autism, 40

boot camps, academic learning, 10
brain growth/development
    claims, 6
    educational advances, 57
    electronic toys, 6
    empty-vessel approach, 19
    mathematical development, 57
    science, 57
Bransford, John D., 61